HEALTHY LIFESTYLES 2
SPHE ACTIVITIES FOR SECOND YEAR STUDENTS

Edel O'Brien

Gill & Macmillan

Gill & Macmillan Ltd
Hume Avenue
Park West
Dublin 12
with associated companies throughout the world
www.gillmacmillan.ie

© Edel O'Brien 2008

Illustrations by Kim Shaw

978 0 7171 4275 0

Print origination in Ireland by Outburst Design

The paper used in this book is made from the wood pulp of managed forests. For every tree felled, at least one tree is planted, thereby renewing natural resources.

Contents

Module 1

Belonging and Integrating

 Looking Back, Looking Forward

 Review of SPHE Class

Make a list of some of the things you learned in first-year SPHE.

_____

_____

_____

_____

_____

Do you think SPHE is an important subject? Why/why not?

_____

_____

_____

_____

What was the most relevant topic you learned in SPHE last year?

_____

_____

_____

_____

In first year you created a class contract. This contract contained the ground rules to help the class work well together.

Class Discussion

Why do you think the class contract is important?

Did the class always stick to the ground rules?

We will now review some of the ground rules that helped the SPHE class to work well last year and adjust the contract if necessary.

Individual Task

What helped the class run well?

_____

_____

_____

What kind of behaviour prevents lessons running smoothly?

_____

_____

What ground rules would you put in place to make sure the SPHE class runs smoothly?

_____

_____

_____

_____

_____

Group Task

Discuss your ideas with the group.

Perhaps others in the group have similar or different views from you. Try to come to an agreement over the ground rules the group would like to implement. Write the agreed ground rules here.

_____

_____

_____

_____

Choose one of your group to share the group's ideas with the rest of the class. The class as a whole must now try to agree to a set of guidelines. Remember: this includes the teacher too!

Once all the members of the class have agreed on the guidelines, perhaps you could design a poster/banner/collage to hang on the wall at the start of each class.

Write the class's agreed guidelines here and ask all your classmates to sign it to show that they support the guidelines.

_____

_____

_____

_____

_____

Signatures:

_____

_____

_____

_____

Review of Last Year

Can you remember this time last year? It was your first week in secondary school. You came from the top year in primary school to the bottom year in secondary school. Everything was new to you and you were faced with the changes and challenges of a new school and a new school year. Change brings with it a lot of uncertainty. Read the following poem about the new boy and try to remember what it felt like to be new and how the present first years may feel.

New Boy

He stood alone in the playground
Scuffed his shoes and stared at the ground
He'd come halfway through term from the Catholic school
On the other side of town.

He'd a brand new blazer and cap on
Polished shoes and neatly cut hair
Blew on his fists, looked up and half smiled
Pretending he didn't care.

And I remembered when I'd been new
And no-one had spoken to me
I'd almost cried as I stood alone
Hiding my misery.

Heart said I should go over
Share a joke or play the fool
But I was scared of looking stupid
In front of the rest of the school.

At break someone said they'd seen him
Crying in the Geography test
And when he came out they pointed and laughed
And I laughed along with the rest.

In my dreams I'd always stood alone
Believing I was the best
But in the cold playground of everyday life
I was no better than the rest.

Gareth Owen

Looking back over the last year, how did you feel at the start of the year?

_____

_____

_____

How did you feel at the end of the year?

_____

_____

_____

What did you like about the year?

_____

_____

What did you dislike about the year?

_____

_____

What things do you need to improve on this year? How do you think you will do this?

_____

_____

_____

How did you feel about your report?

_____

_____

Looking back on first year helps you to reflect on your achievements: it also helps you to make improvements in second year. Perhaps you were disappointed with your report or you got into trouble more than you would have wished, or perhaps you would like to have got more involved in extra-curricular activities.

The start of second year is a great opportunity for you to set goals and to make decisions about what you want to achieve in the year ahead.

→ Goal Setting

Individual Work

Imagine it is ten years from now. What would you like people to say about you?

_____

_____

What would you like a close friend to say about you?

_____

_____

What would you like your parents to say about you?

_____

_____

This exercise helps you to focus on what's important to you. It's only by realising what matters to you that you can make steps towards achieving your goals. By knowing exactly what you want to achieve you can plan and concentrate your efforts on achieving it. This is called goal setting. Setting goals can be extremely motivating. As you get older your goals will change and you will have to adjust them.

In order to achieve your long-term goals you have to have short-term goals. A long-term goal is far in the future, for example 'I want to do well in my Junior Certificate'. A short-term goal could be to get good grades in your class exams.

Class Discussion

What happens if you have no goals?

_____

_____

Individual Task

Can you think of a time in your life where you achieved something?

_____

_____

How did you feel after you achieved it?

_____

_____

Below are examples of goals people might set in different areas of their lives.
Can you write down some goals for your own life? They can be short-term
or long-term. Make sure that they are goals that you genuinely want.

Exercise	Keep fit and get in shape		**Exercise**	
Attitude	Control my temper		**Attitude**	
Education	Get a good Junior Certificate		**Education**	
Home Life	Get on better with my brother		**Home Life**	
Leisure time	Meet new friends		**Leisure time**	
Career	Go to college and get a good job		**Career**	

Goals are set on a number of different levels.
- First you need to have in your mind what you want to achieve. For example, 'I want to do better at Geography'.
- Then you decide what steps you need to take to achieve your goal, e.g. 'practise my diagrams', 'revise regularly', 'study before exams', 'do my homework', 'get help from a friend'.
- What could prevent you achieving your goal? Not reading over material from class regularly, not practising diagrams. Not paying attention in class.
- When do you hope to achieve your goal? Christmas exam.

Your goals do not have to be related to school, they can be about learning to play a musical instrument, improving your basketball skills or changing the way you behave.

Now set your own goal for this year. Make sure it is something you actually want to achieve. When you have achieved your goal, enjoy it – reward yourself if you wish.

 Useful Website

www.mindtools.com

The goal I want to achieve is:

_____

_____

_____

What do I need to do to achieve my goal?

_____

_____

_____

What could prevent me from achieving my goal?

_____

_____

_____

When do I hope to achieve my goal?

_____

_____

 # Group Work

Throughout our lives we work with others in groups or as part of a team – at school, in sports, in our family, or as part of an organisation or committee.

What are the benefits of group work or team work?

_____

_____

Write about a time you were part of a group. What was your role in the group? Did the group work well together? Why?

Using the following headings, write down what could help a group work well together and what could prevent a group working well together.

	Helps the group work well	Prevents the group working well
Particpation		
Co-operation		
Leadership		
Making decisions		

 **Family Ties**

In the spaces provided write down what you like about your family and what you dislike about them.

I like	I dislike

Class Discussion

How did you feel about doing this activity?

Did you have more likes or dislikes?

 Relationships with Parents

'My parents are so strict'; 'My mother is driving me mad.' Can you relate to these comments?

During adolescence you start to feel more grown up and have more responsibilities, not only in school but also at home. It can be frustrating for many teenagers that even though they feel like an adult, they are not given the freedom they would like. Sometimes you just wish your parents would give you some privacy. All these factors can result in arguments at home.

Some teenagers are lucky enough to have parents they can talk to and confide in, but some may feel that their parents are out of touch and that they could never talk to them about anything important. More than likely things will get easier as you get older, but you don't have to wait until then to improve your relationship with your parents: there are things you can do now. Remember, your parents are not deliberately trying to make life difficult for you. They worry and care about you and don't want you to come to any harm. It is important to talk to your parents.

Individual Work

Has your relationship with your parents/carers changed since you were younger? How? Why?

_____

_____

_____

Group Work

Write down the things you argue with your parents about most often. Some suggestions are:

1 They keep asking you to tidy your bedroom.

2 They don't like your friends or boyfriend/girlfriend.

3 They think you're not working hard enough at school.

_____

_____

_____

_____

_____

_____

_____

In each case discuss how arguments could be avoided.

1 _____

_____

2 _____

_____

3 _____

_____

4 _____

_____

5 _____

_____

Here are some guidelines to help you get on better with your parents or carers.

- If they do not allow you to do something don't get wound up and lose your temper. Parents will not react positively to screaming and door-slamming.
- Wait until you're calm to talk things through.
- Try to see things from their point of view. Ask questions. Ask them to explain why you are not allowed go to the party all your friends are going to. Listen to what they are worried about. Give your side and try to dispel some of their fears. Try to come up with a compromise.
- Take time to chat to your parents. Spend time with them – even if it's just eating a meal together or sitting watching a DVD when you're all at home.
- Show your parents you can behave responsibly. Keep your bedroom tidy. Do some household chores without being asked.
- Don't tell lies – if they catch you out they won't trust you again.

Weekly Task

Decide on one thing you could do this week to help improve your relationship with your parents or carers.

 Being Responsible

- Keeping your room tidy.
- Washing and ironing clothes.
- Looking after a younger brother or sister.
- Returning something you borrowed.

These are examples of household tasks or responsibilities. In order for a household to run well and for a family to get on well together it is important that household responsibilities are shared out. Arguments sometimes happen when one person feels they are doing more than another.

Write down some of the tasks and responsibilities necessary in family life. Write down which member of your family is responsible for each one.

_____

_____

_____

_____

What responsibilities do you have at home? Has your role changed as you have grown older?

_____

_____

_____

_____

How could you ensure that the tasks in your house are more evenly distributed?

_____

_____

_____

Joan

Joan turned the key in her front door after a hard day at work in the hospital. She was looking forward to getting home, putting down the shopping and relaxing for an hour. As she came through the door she could hear the twins arguing. Susan had taken John's CD. On hearing his mother coming in, John roars, 'Maaaam, Susan took my CD and lost it.' This is the last thing Joan wants. She walks into the kitchen to find it is a mess. Sam is sitting on a chair watching television. Joan says to Sam in a sharp voice, 'Get up, Sam, and clean this kitchen.' Sam protests that he did not dirty it. The twins then come into the kitchen, and John says, 'What's for dinner, Mam? I'm starving!' Joan is so annoyed.

Class Discussion

Would you describe this as a normal family situation?
What are the main cause of arguments in families?
What do you think is causing the upset in this family?
How could these arguments have been avoided?

Role Plays

Characters: you will need three or more characters to create a family situation.
Roles: agree on the part each person will play in the family.
Re-enact some of the following family situations:

1 A parent is not happy with the housework being done by the children in the family.
2 Daughter arrives home from a night out later than told.
3 Daughter aged 14 is going out with a boy of 16.
4 Son has not done his homework, his friends call and ask him to come out.
5 Sister teases her brother about a girl he fancies.

Module 2

Self Management: A Sense of Purpose

What Motivates Me?

My mother said she would give me €100 for every A I got in my summer exams so I am really going to study hard this year.

I study hard at school because I want a career I enjoy and I want to have a good salary.

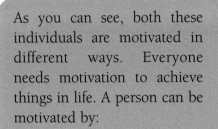

As you can see, both these individuals are motivated in different ways. Everyone needs motivation to achieve things in life. A person can be motivated by:

- praise from parents
- getting a qualification
- gaining respect and admiration from friends and family
- the pride they get from completing a challenge
- enjoyment and satisfaction in doing an activity, e.g. solving crosswords, doing mathematical problems or being involved in sport
- the joy of making a difference in someone else's life
- achieving a lifetime dream.

What do you think motivates the following people?

- county hurler
- coach of an average football team
- Junior Cert student
- charity worker
- professional soccer player
- child learning to ride his/her bike.

What motivates you to work hard at school?

_____

_____

_____

_____

_____

**Think about an activity you do in your spare time.
What motivates you to do it well?**

_____

_____

_____

_____

 # Study Skills

The key to good study is to regularly revisit what you learn. With this in mind, let's recap the study techniques and skills you learned in first year. For each section fill in what you already know.

You might like to go back to the first-year book to fill in anything you can't remember; or ask your teacher for help.

Group Work

Describe a good place to study.

- Well lit
- _____
- _____
- _____
- _____
- _____
- _____

Write down some of the ways you can organise yourself for study.

- Have a daily and weekly timetable.

- Tidy your bag.

- _____

- _____

- _____

- _____

- _____

Using good study techniques is more helpful than just studying hard. Can you remember any techniques you learned last year? Give some examples.

- _____

- _____

- _____

- _____

- _____

What is the best way to take notes from your textbook?

_____

_____

_____

Imagine you have to study a section of your textbook. What is the most effective way to do this?

Step 1: Jot down what you already know

Step 2: _____

Step 3: _____

→ **Study Groups**

Did you find revising study strategies as a group was a good way to revise? Why?

_____

_____

Group study is when a group of friends or classmates get together to study. This can be a very helpful way to revise because:

1 it is easier to ask questions in a small group

2 in a subject like maths you can help each other solve difficult problems

3 talking aloud about what you are studying can help you understand and remember it

4 another group member may know something you are unsure of

5 studying alone can be boring: working in a group can make it more fun

6 if you have to meet a group to study you are more committed: you don't want to let the others down.

Second Year Study Timetable

In first year you learned how to create a study timetable. This year you may have fewer subjects or you might be doing a sport on a different evening. Fill in the study timetable below for second year. Make a photocopy and stick it on your wall to remind yourself.

	Leisure Activity	Subjects	Times
Monday			
Tuesday			
Wednesday			
Thursday			
Friday			
Saturday			
Sunday			

 # Taking Tests

Sometimes, when you do a test in class, even though you studied hard, you don't get the result you want. Below are a couple of common mistakes people make when taking tests. Can you add some more?

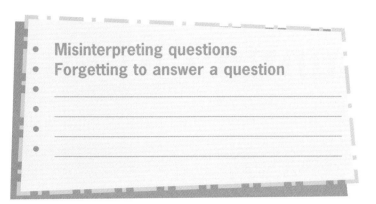

- Misinterpreting questions
- Forgetting to answer a question
- _____
- _____
- _____
- _____

Useful Websites

www.howtostudy.com
www.kidshealth.org

There is a system for taking tests which can help you do better: it's the DETER strategy. Each letter reminds you of what to do in the test. (Adapted from www.howtostudy.com.)

D = Directions
- Read all the instructions very carefully.

E = Examine
- Examine the test to see how much you have to do.

T = Time
- Once you have examined the test decide how much time you will spend on each section.
- For example, a maths exam is two and a half hours long and you have to answer six questions. Each question carries the same number of marks. You need to decide how long you should spend on each question. Remember to leave five minutes at the start and five minutes at the end to read over the paper. So:
  Time for six questions = 150 mins
  Reading the test = 10 mins
  Time left to do all the questions = 140 mins
  So each question gets 23 mins.
- Look at how many marks are given for each question.
- Spend the most time on questions with the most marks. You would not write the same amount for a six-mark question and a twenty-mark question.
- If you have spent the assigned time on a question you need to move on. You will have got as many marks as you can on it.

E = Easiest
- Answer the questions you find easiest first. This will help you to relax.

R = Review
- If you have planned your time properly you will have time to read back over the exam and correct any errors.

Module 3

Assertive Communication

In first year you learned about the difference between assertive, aggressive and passive behaviour. Look at the table to help you recap what each means.

Passive	Assertive	Aggressive
You do... • rely on others to guess what you want • hope that you will get what you want • 'sit on' your feelings • sigh, sulk, hint, wish ... • feel trampled on	**You do...** • ask for what you want • behave openly and directly • believe in yourself • ask confidently and without undue anxiety • look for 'win-win' situations	**You do...** • try to get what you want in any way that works • often cause bad feelings in others • threaten, cajole, use sarcasm, bully, manipulate, fight
You don't... • ask for what you want • express your feelings • usually get what you want • feel good about yourself	**You don't...** • violate other people's rights • expect other people to guess what you want • freeze with anxiety	**You don't...** • respect the fact that others have rights too • look for 'win-win' situations

Thanks for letting me borrow it.

Thanks...

Thanks for letting me borrow it.

Please could you mend the puncture before giving it back?

Thanks for letting me borrow it.

What have you done to my bike? You are NEVER borrowing it again!

Decide whether each of the following is assertive, aggressive or passive behaviour.

1 You purchase a coat. After returning home you notice it is ripped under the arm. When you return to the store the shop assistant claims you damaged it. You respond by saying:

 a) 'The cheek of you, how dare you speak to me like that? I should know – I bought it.'

 b) 'I can assure you I did not damage this item. I am in my full rights to receive a refund.'

 c) 'OK, I suppose I'll have to keep it.'

2 You are hanging out with your friends on your estate. A neighbour comes out of her house and asks you to move on, as you are keeping her child awake. You respond by saying

 a) 'We're very sorry, we didn't realise.'

 b) 'Get a life! It's a free country – you can't tell us what to do.'

 c) 'It's not our fault we have nowhere else to go' (under your breath).

3 Your teacher finds your name carved on the desk. You have not done it. She tells you that you will receive a detention for it. You respond by saying:

 a) 'I always get blamed! This school is such a dump.'

 b) 'What day will I do the detention?'

 c) 'Miss, I honestly did not damage the desk. I would never do something like that.'

4 You are going to a disco. You are wearing a new jacket. When you meet your friend she tells you she does not think it suits you. You respond by saying:

 a) 'What do you know? Look at the state of what you're wearing!'

 b) 'Thanks, but I really like it on me.'

 c) 'I'll go home and change.'

ANNA
CAFFREY

How do you think you would react in each situation above?
Write about a time when you were:

Assertive:

_____

_____

Aggressive:

_____

_____

Passive:

_____

_____

How did you feel afterwards?

_____

_____

_____

Could you have done or said anything differently?

_____

_____

_____

Would it have helped?

_____

_____

_____

Learning to be assertive can benefit you in many areas of your life. It can help you :

> 1 express positive feelings well
> 2 express negative feelings well
> 3 stand up for your rights.

Assertiveness Quiz:

How assertive are you?

For each section tick the box that applies to you.

How good are you at:

	Very Good	Good	Average	Not Good
Expressing positive feelings				
Telling someone you appreciate them	❑	❑	❑	❑
Giving compliments	❑	❑	❑	❑
Receiving compliments without feeling embarrassed	❑	❑	❑	❑
Starting conversations	❑	❑	❑	❑
Expressing negative feelings				
Showing annoyance	❑	❑	❑	❑
Showing hurt	❑	❑	❑	❑
Standing up for your rights				
Making complaints	❑	❑	❑	❑
Refusing requests, i.e. saying no	❑	❑	❑	❑
Giving your opinion	❑	❑	❑	❑
Refusing to be put down	❑	❑	❑	❑

(Source: Health Skills Unit – Counselling and Career Development Unit)

Tips on How to be Assertive

- Use assertive body language, stand or sit straight, have a firm but not aggressive expression, keep your voice calm and not whiney. Use eye contact.
- Use clear direct statements such as 'Would you please return my top?' rather than 'Would you mind returning my top?'
- Say what you have to say and stick to it.
- When refusing a request say no clearly. If you are unsure, don't make a rushed decision – say you will get back to them.

 **Useful Website**

hhtp://campus.umr.edu

Physical Health

 ## Body Care and Body Image

What do body image and hygiene have in common?

Think about what you feel like after you play a match or when you've been camping. Don't you get all dirty, sweaty and stinky? What's the first thing you want to do? Usually have a long hot shower. After the shower you usually say, 'Ah, I feel so much better now.' The reason for this is that when you feel good about your body physically, you feel better about yourself. When you get up in the morning and have a shower or a wash before going to school you feel much better for the day.

Our body is constantly regenerating itself. Nails grow and fall off. Skin is constantly being shed and regenerated. Hair grows and falls out. You help that process by bathing, brushing, shaving, moisturising, exfoliating and protecting.

Group Task

In groups recap the principles of hygiene you learned in first year. One has been done for you.

How to avoid body odour	*Wash under your arms every day.*
Skin care	
Dental care	
Hair care	

 # Posture and Body Image

Posture means the way you hold your body when you are standing, sitting or walking. Having a good posture can contribute to looking and feeling good about yourself. Walking with your head up and your shoulders back can help you to look better and feel more confident.

Which of the people below have good posture?

Class Activity

Everyone in the class gets up off their seat and walks around.

First walk the way you normally do.

On the teacher's command straighten your back, push back your shoulders and hold your head up.

Class Discussion

How did you feel doing this activity?

Tips for Maintaining Good Posture

Do you find your schoolbag is weighing you down? When a heavy bag, like a schoolbag filled with books, is incorrectly placed on the shoulders, it can put excessive strain on the back, which can cause back pain and affects your posture.

It is important to:

1 choose the right size bag

2 use both shoulder straps

3 put in only what you really need

4 look for a bag with wider straps – they distribute the load more evenly

5 wear the bag high on your back.

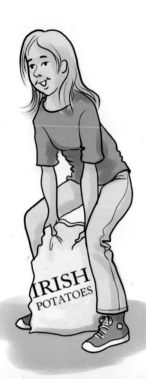

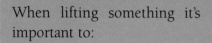

When lifting something it's important to:

- lift only what you are able to lift safely
- bend your hips and knees so that they do the work, not your back
- keep a firm grip on what you are lifting
- hold what you are lifting close to your body.

 Suntanning and Body Image

Many people nowadays feel that having a suntan is essential if they want to look and feel good. It is important to remember that getting an all-over tan can have damaging effects on your skin and on your health. Read what Claire has to say.

Claire

I'm 17 and I have been using sunbeds since I was 14. In my opinion white pasty skin is so unattractive. I've heard about all the dangers but who cares? I could get knocked down crossing the road tomorrow. At least I would die with a nice tan. Everything seems to be bad for you these days. I say go out there, look good and have fun!

Class Discussion

What do you think of Claire's opinion?

What is your opinion of sunbeds?

How important is having a tan to young people?

Are we risking vanity for our health?

 ## What is Sun Damage?

Sun damage is over-exposure to the sun's rays. The sun produces two types of ultraviolet rays, UVA and UVB. Both types can penetrate deep into the skin, causing damage. Brainstorm as many effects of the sun as you can.

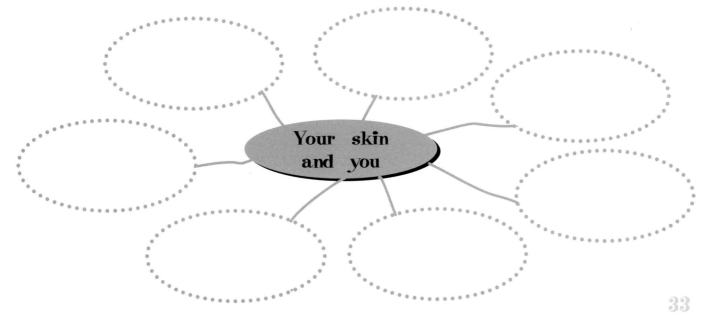

Your skin and you

How safe are you in the sun?

Whether you are at home or abroad the sun's rays can burn you severely. It makes your skin hot and sore at the time, but even more important, in the long term sun damage can cause cancer. Despite this knowledge many Irish people do not take the issue of safety in the sun seriously.

Complete the questionnaire below.

Sunburn Quiz:

1 Have you ever been sunburned?

Yes ☐

No ☐

2 If yes, how often have you been sunburned?

Rarely ☐

Every summer ☐

Every time I go out in the sun ☐

3 How severe was the sunburn?

Very severe ☐

Very mild ☐

Quite sore ☐

4 How long would you sit in the sun without covering up?

Less than 30 minutes ☐

A few hours ☐

As long as it takes to get a quick tan ☐

5 How often would you apply sunscreen?

Rarely ☐

Never ☐

Sometimes ☐

Always ☐

6 What type of sunscreen would you use in Ireland?

SPF 15+ ❏

SPF 8 or less ❏

Oil ❏

No sunscreen ❏

7 Sunscreen should be applied:

When your skin starts to get red ❏

Once, before you go out in the sun ❏

Once every two hours and after swimming ❏

8 A sunscreen of SPF 15+ means:

You can stay out in the sun 15 times longer ❏

It provides 15 times your natural protection ❏

You are protected for 15 minutes in the sun ❏

9 Ultraviolet radiation is strongest:

All day ❏

Between 10am and 1pm ❏

Between 11am and 4pm ❏

10 How often do you wear a hat in the sun?

Never ❏

Rarely ❏

Usually ❏

Always ❏

Sun damage: the facts

You don't have to be a sun worshipper to be at risk from the effects of the sun. People with pale skin are particularly at risk, but it is important that people of all skin types protect their skin from the sun. Damage to our skin is permanent, irreversible and builds up over time, so it is important to protect our skin when you are young.

The effects of sun damage include:

- premature ageing (wrinkles)
- sagging skin
- broken blood vessels
- sunburn
- cancer
- disfigurement
- peeling
- skin thickening.

Despite the risks, Irish people continue to be under- cautious. The Irish Cancer Society believes Irish people do not take safety in the sun seriously. According to the Health Promotion Unit skin cancer is the most common form of cancer in Ireland and six out of ten Irish people use sunbeds to get a base tan. Most Irish people see sunscreen as sufficient protection in the sun.

Here are some guidelines on how to protect yourself from the sun.

- Stay out of the sun between 11am and 3pm.
- Cover up – sunscreen is not always sufficient.
- Wear sunscreen with a suitable SPF (sun protection factor) and reapply it every two hours or after swimming and sweating.
- The SPF of a product tells you how long you can stay in the sun. For example, SPF 15 gives you 15 times your normal protection.
- Watch the sunburn forecast.
- Wear a hat and sunglasses at all times in the sun.

Remember: you can get sunburned through clouds, in the snow, and on a breezy day.

There are so many great tanning products around these days, why not use them?

 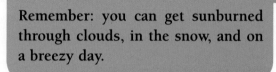 **Useful Websites**

www.irishhealth.ie
www.bodywhys.ie
www.lifebytes.gov.uk/safety/safe_sun.html
www.clearasil.com

 # Feeling Unwell

Can you think of the last time you had an upset stomach, a cold or flu? Do you know what made you sick? Diseases and infections are caused by harmful micro-organisms such as bacteria and viruses. These are more commonly referred to as germs or bugs.

 ## Bacteria

Bacteria are tiny rod-shaped cells that can only be seen under a microscope. Bacteria are found in the air, in the soil, in water and in the human body. Some bacteria are useful but some are harmful and cause diseases and infections in humans. Some of the health problems caused by bacteria are:

- sore throat
- food poisoning
- pimples
- gum infections
- stomach bugs.

 ## Viruses

Viruses are tiny particles which can only be seen under an electron microscope. Viruses can only survive in living cells. They cause illnesses such as:

- colds
- flu
- measles
- mumps
- chicken pox
- AIDS.

Bacteria and viruses can be spread through:

- the air, e.g. through sneezing and coughing
- poor hygiene standards
- body contact (e.g. cold sores can be passed on in this way)
- food, e.g. food that's past its sell-by date
- drinking dirty water.

Look at the picture below and mark on it the possible sources of infection.

Class Discussion

How can we stop the spread of infection?

The best way to deal with infection is to avoid it in the first place. Insist on the highest standards of hygiene, especially where food is concerned.

Here are some important guidelines on preparing food.

1 Always check the sell-by date when buying a product.

2 Always wash your hands after handling food.

3 Do not refreeze defrosted food.

4 Do not use the same knife for cutting raw meat and other food.

5 Reheat food thoroughly.

6 Make sure surfaces are clean before you start preparing food.

7 Store food in the fridge or freezer when necessary.

8 Do not leave food uncovered.

9 Tie your hair back when cooking.

Group Task

Write down a list of hygiene standards under the following headings.

Washing your hands (e.g. wash your hands before eating)

_____

_____

_____

Flies and food

_____

_____

_____

Cuts and open wounds

_____

_____

_____

Pets

_____

_____

_____

Eating fruit and vegetables

_____

_____

_____

Coughing and sneezing

_____

_____

_____

How Your Body Fights Infection

Your skin is the first line of defence in fighting disease. White blood cells are the second line of defence. White cells destroy germs and bacteria that enter the body. Your body also makes antibodies which attack germs and destroy disease.

Sometimes your body needs antibiotics and vaccinations to help fight disease. Antibiotics cannot treat viruses, they can only be used to treat bacterial infections. Vaccines are used to protect against viruses.

Vaccines

Vaccines are used to protect people against diseases such as measles, mumps, rubella, tuberculosis and tetanus. When a person is vaccinated a small, harmless amount of the virus that causes the disease is injected into the bloodstream. The body produces antibodies to fight the virus that causes the real disease. For example, if you receive the measles vaccination a small amount of the virus is injected into the body. So if you come in contact with measles later, your body will recognise the virus and prevent you from getting the disease.

What to do if You Feel Unwell

Everyone feels unwell from time to time. You might get flu, a head cold or sunburn. These are not normally serious or life-threatening, so they are called minor ailments. You can take a medicine or use other remedies to treat the ailment, but remember: if the symptoms are severe and last for a long time, you should go to a doctor.

Project

Below is a list of minor ailments. Choose any three from the list. Research the symptoms and treatment of each ailment. If possible, find out about alternative (natural) remedies.

- colds
- flu
- cough
- headache
- hay fever
- indigestion

- muscular pain
- cold sores
- athlete's foot
- headlice
- dandruff
- sunburn

- sore throat
- vomiting
- diarrhoea
- earache
- toothache

Minor Ailments	Symptoms	Treatments

If we are feeling unwell, we can seek the advice of friends or family members. Health articles in newspapers and magazines also give remedies for minor ailments. If you are feeling unwell your pharmacist will be able to advise you and recommend a medicine if appropriate. It is important that you tell the pharmacist your symptoms. The pharmacist will also advise you on whether you need to see a doctor. (Source: 'Managing your Minor Ailments Effectively', Health Promotion Unit.)

 Taking medicines

- Always follow the instructions you are given on the information sheet.
- Do not take more than the recommended dose.
- Do not take medicines that have been prescribed for another person.
- Do not take two or more products containing paracetamol together. If you are unsure whether a product contains paracetamol, ask your pharmacist.

Invite the local pharmacist to visit your school to talk about minor ailments.

Visiting the Doctor

If you do have to go to your doctor:

- You can usually choose whether you want to see a male or female doctor.
- Be sure to tell him/her exactly what your symptoms are.
- If you feel he/she has misunderstood you, repeat yourself.
- If you do not understand the doctor's diagnosis don't be afraid to ask him/her to explain or ask a parent to speak to the doctor.

 # Medical History

The following information may be helpful if you ever visit the doctor or an emergency department in hospital. Ask a parent for help if necessary.

What is your blood group? _____

Have you had a tetanus injection? _____

Have you any allergies? _____

Have you ever had a general anaesthetic? _____

Have you had any serious illnesses? _____

Have you ever have an allergic reaction
to a medication? _____

Role Play

In pairs, choose a minor ailment and role play a visit to the doctor.

Staying Well

The best way to deal with minor ailments is to avoid getting them in the first place. Eating healthily, regular exercise, good hygiene, not smoking and regular check-ups can help.

It is always important to keep important contact numbers in case of emergency.

In the case of an emergency dial 999 or 112 and ask for ambulance, fire or Gardai.

Make a list of other important numbers.

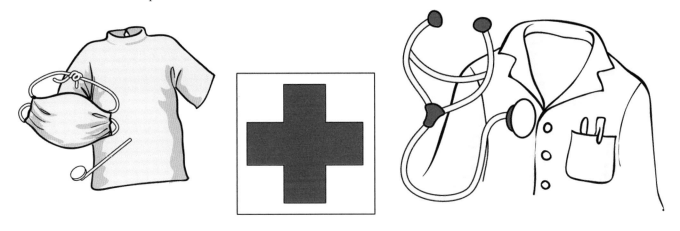

Doctor:	Name _____	Tel _____
Local Hospital:	_____	Tel _____
Pharmacist:	_____	Tel _____
Dentist:	_____	Tel _____
Others:	_____	Tel _____
	_____	Tel _____
	_____	Tel _____

Sometimes people suffer from illnesses their whole life. Some illnesses are hereditary (i.e. they are passed down from one generation to the next). In most cases, if the correct medication is taken the illness can be controlled and the person can lead a normal life. An illness such as meningitis may only occur once, but if not detected in time it can prove fatal.

Project Work

Choose an illness to research. You can choose an illness that has affected you or someone you know. You can ask a doctor for advice if you wish.

Choose from the list below or pick a different illness. Include in your findings:

- a description of the disease
- symptoms of the disease
- causes
- treatment.

Diseases/illnesses to research:

- meningitis
- asthma
- epilepsy
- diabetes.

Make a presentation to the class on your findings.

Helpful Websites

www.kidshealth.org
www.vhi.ie
www.irishhealth.ie

Module 5

Friendship

The Changing Nature of Friendship

Look back on your primary school and first year. Have the friends you have made changed or stayed the same?

_____

_____

_____

Why do you think changes have occurred in your friendships?

_____

_____

_____

Do you believe the friends you have now will stay your friends forever?

_____

_____

_____

Throughout our lives we will become close to people and make good friends. These friendships, however, may change as our lives change. People sometimes grow apart as the interests in their lives change. Sometimes this is inevitable and you just have to go your separate ways. It is important to choose friends who are right for you and who are loyal to you. From the list below circle out what makes a good friend.

A friend is someone who:

- **stands up for you**
- **is fun to be around**
- **remembers your birthday**
- **is good looking**
- **is reliable**
- **always returns your texts**
- **buys things for you**
- **picks you up when you're feeling down**
- **listens to you and advises you**
- **shares the same interests**
- **you can share private information with**
- **respects your decisions**
- **pressurises you into making decisions.**

What qualities do you have as a friend?

_____

_____

_____

_____

Bullying

As you learned in first year, bullying is a deliberate, repeated and hurtful attack on a person. Bullying can happen in many different ways. Can you match each type of bullying with a word or phrase that describes it?

lack of concentration   hitting   criticising

NAME-CALLING

shoving

spreading rumours   making threats

teasing

sending insulting images over the internet   sending threatening messages by mobile phone

excluding   making intimidating gestures

insulting   kicking

ignoring

Physical	Verbal	Emotional

Non-Verbal	E-Bullying

Group Task

Write down some comments that can be hurtful or put people down.

Hurtful comments:

_____

_____

_____

_____

_____

Questions

How do you think each of these comments affects the person?

_____

_____

_____

How do you think the bully feels?

_____

_____

_____

What could you do if you heard someone saying these things to another person?

_____

_____

_____

What is the effect of making comments like these?

_____

_____

_____

 # Cyber Bullying

Cyber bullying is when a person uses electronic types of equipment such as mobile phones and computers to bully their victim repeatedly over time. Unfortunately this adds another worrying dimension to bullying as the bully can target their victim in the privacy of their own home. Examples include:

- **text bullying** – sending threatening or unwelcome texts
- **picture/video clip bullying** – sending pictures or videos that may upset or embarrass a person. Could include recordings of an attack
- **phone call bullying** – making unwanted and threatening calls
- **email bullying** – using emails to send upsetting messages
- **hate sites** – websites dedicated to humiliating someone.

Class Discussion

Do you think teenage internet blog sites (e.g. Bebo) could be used for bullying?

Have you heard of someone being bullied through video clips?

49

Bullies Made my Life Hell

When Aoife changed schools she was excited about all the new friends she'd make. Until she met Gemma and things turned very nasty ...

I was so nervous about starting secondary school as all my friends were going to another school. Luckily I made friends quite quickly, but all the girls I became friendly with had known each other since Primary, so I felt like a bit of an outsider.

I could tell from the word go that Gemma was the ringleader of the gang. She's really pretty and all the girls acted like they were almost in awe of her. She could also be really bitchy, even about her own friends, which worried me because I could only imagine what she might say about me. But I really liked the other girls and soon enough I started meeting them at the weekends instead of my old friends. I tried to bring a few of my old pals out with them a couple of times but it was really awkward, so I decided to keep them separate from then on.

Last summer started off brilliantly. I met the girls every day and we'd go shopping, hang out in the park or at each others' houses. We started hanging around with a group of lads, so people were getting it together. I fancied this guy James and we immediately clicked. Everyone was talking about how cute we were together and that it was so obvious that we liked each other. We got an awful slagging but it was funny at the same time, and I kind of liked all the attention.

It was around this time that I noticed Gemma being really off with me. Apparently she really fancied James and she didn't like that James and I were getting on so well. It was only after I snogged James that the rest of the girls turned on me. They were horrible to me and they soon stopped asking me to go to the park or answering my texts or phone calls.

One day I got a text from a number I didn't know that read, 'Gemma's with James now, jealous?'

I couldn't believe it. I rang into the voicemail to find out who it was but it was just a machine recording. I got a good few more texts like that during the summer but I never responded.

I also started hanging out with my old friends again. They knew I'd fallen out with the girls and I was just so grateful that they were sill talking to me after how I had treated them.

I was dreading going back to school after the holidays and I was right to have been worried. The girls had changed completely. They'd 'accidentally' bump into me in the corridors, call me names any time I'd walk past them and they wrote things about me on the doors in the girls' loos. When they were feeling really brave they'd trip me up or throw things at me. They'd also fill my locker with mouldy fruit and then stand near it, complaining about the horrible smell and saying that I didn't wash.

It continued like that for about three months, until eventually I couldn't take any more. I broke down to my mum one night and she went straight to the Principal. The girls got into loads of trouble and there was a big thing about bullying in school. Gemma and her gang totally ignored me from that day on, which I didn't mind at all. For a few weeks afterwards I didn't really have anyone to hang around with (and sometimes I wondered whether I'd done the right thing) but I eventually made some really good friends and I'm really happy now. I now know that those girls are just weak and pathetic bullies and I'm glad I spoke out about them. I'm only sorry I didn't do it sooner.

© *Kiss* magazine

1 Why do you think Gemma bullied Aoife?

2 Write down the different forms of bullying in this story.

3 How did this experience affect Aoife's life?

4 If you witnessed this bullying behaviour, what could you do?

5 What could you do in your school if you were being bullied or you knew someone who was being bullied?

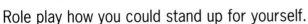

Role Play

Imagine you are Aoife and these girls are bullying you.
Role play how you could stand up for yourself.

Class Discussion

Could a boy be bullied in the same way as Aoife? Do you think there is a difference in the way males and females are bullied?

 Text Message Bullying

What should you do if you are receiving threatening or upsetting messages?

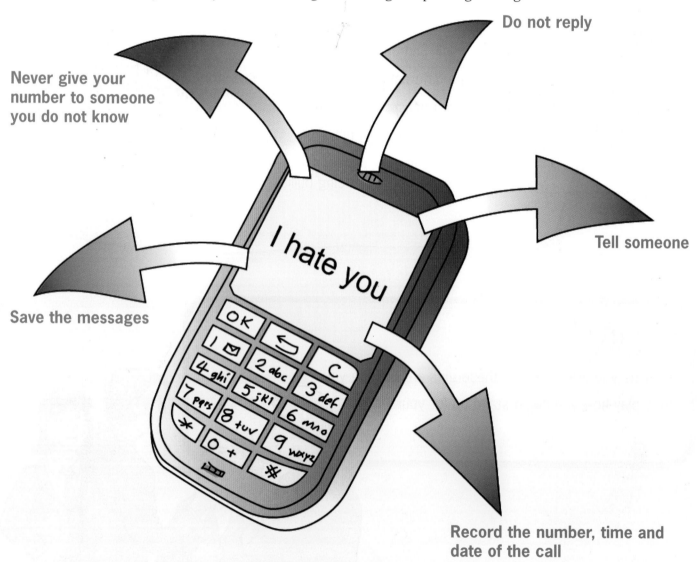

Never give your number to someone you do not know

Do not reply

Tell someone

Save the messages

Record the number, time and date of the call

If you are being bullied:

- tell someone you trust
- try not to use violence – it can make the situation worse
- talk calmly and stand up for yourself
- try not to show you are upset or angry
- keep a diary so you can remember your story
- get support from your friends
- try not to be alone in places where you can be picked on.

Remember – be a friend to someone you feel is getting a hard time. This may mean befriending someone who is not in your group or not joining in with the others when they are laughing. Imagine you were the person being bullied: would you like to be treated this way? A kind word of support can be very helpful.

 ## Useful Websites

www.news.bbc.co.uk/cbbcnews
www.dfes.gov.uk/bullying/cyberbullying
www.kidshealth.org
www.there4me.com

Module 6

Influences and Decisions

Positive and Negative Influences

As you learned in first year there are many people who influence our lives and the decisions we make. Sometimes we are unaware of their influence.

How would the following people influence your decision to drink?

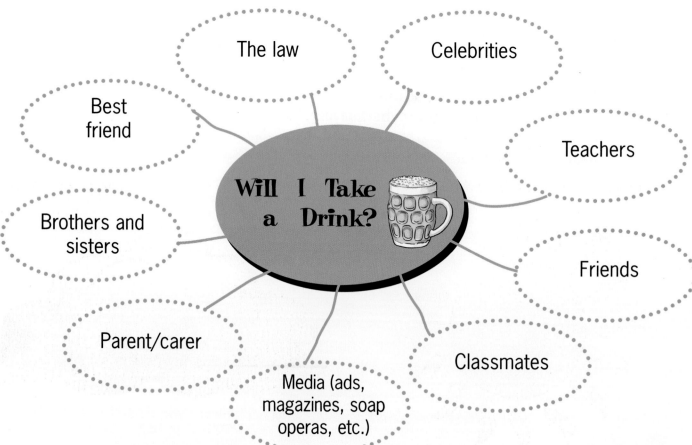

The law

Celebrities

Best friend

Teachers

Brothers and sisters

Will I Take a Drink?

Friends

Parent/carer

Classmates

Media (ads, magazines, soap operas, etc.)

Write about a decision you made recently. Who influenced this decision?

_____

_____

_____

_____

_____

Influences can be either positive or negative. They are positive if they help us to get on better in life and negative if they prevent us from doing as well as we should. Sometimes both influences act together, for example fame can be a positive influence in a person's life if it helps them to develop their career but a negative influence if they lose their privacy because they are constantly being followed by paparazzi (e.g. Princess Diana).

Below are some examples of positive and negative influences in a person's life.

Positive Influences	Negative influences
My father teaching me how to swim	Underage drinking
My friend helping me through a difficult time	Friends who discouraged me from studying
Doing well in exams and getting the course I wanted	A bully who made life in primary school difficult

In the sun below write all the positive influences in your life so far and in the cloud write all the negative influences.

Class Activity

Perhaps there is a negative influence in your life that affects or upsets you. There is no point in holding negative feelings inside, so write the influence on a label and attach it to a balloon. Everyone in the class should go outside and release their own balloon: this will help you to get rid of negative feelings.

Making Decisions

Decisions, decisions ... We all make a lot of decisions every day, most of them trivial, for example, what shall I eat for breakfast? Will I wear the blue or the red top? Which suits me better? These decisions require very little thought, as we do not have to think about the consequences of our actions. Sometimes, however, we have to make serious decisions in life, because our actions will have more important consequences. For example, should I take a lift from someone I know has been drinking? Consider this: you are at a party and your parents expect you home by twelve o'clock. It's now after twelve and you cannot get a taxi. Your friend's brother offers to give you and your friend a lift home. You are sure you saw him drinking earlier on, but you really need to get home. What should you do?

When we are making decisions, there are usually a number of options available to us and we need to consider all the options carefully. The wrong decision can have serious consequences.

Decision	Options	Possible Consequences
Will I take the lift?	Take the lift	Pulled over by the guards Car accident Death Living with the death of another person
	Don't take the lift	Late home Punished by parents You won't be injured in car crash
	Ring your parents for a lift home and explain the situation	Parents annoyed at first – but they will understand You are safe from harm

Group Work

Think of three important decisions a person may have to make in their life. Fill in the grid below.

Decision	Options	Possible Consequences
1.		
2.		
3.		

A

 # Decision-making Styles

Not all decisions have serious consequences, but there are many decisions in life which are difficult and can cause us problems. For example, what subjects should I choose for my Leaving Cert? People make decisions in different ways: some people are very good at making decisions (whether or not the decision is good is another matter) and can make their mind up quickly; others agonise for ages over what decision to make. Sometimes people can ask too many other people for advice and this can make the decision even more difficult. The important thing is to make the best decision for you, one that you don't regret. Spending too much time pondering over your decision can be stressful.

Here are some steps that will help you make good decisions.

1 Pinpoint the decision you have to make and gather information from friends, family, the internet, etc. For example, what subjects shall I choose for Leaving Certificate? Ask the career guidance teacher for help.

2 Identify your options

- What subjects are available?

- Is this a subject you would enjoy?

- Could you study this subject outside school?

3 List the advantages and disadvantages of choosing each option. Consider what is important to you.

Advantages:

- it can help you get you a good career/a well-paid job

- you like the teacher

- you enjoy the subject

- you will need it to do the course you want in college

- your friends are doing it

- you did well at it in your Junior Cert

- the school has good facilities for studying the subject

- it will help you get the job you want

- your older brother did it

- it's supposed to be easy to get a good grade in that subject

- it would get you easy points.

Disadvantages:

- you don't like the teacher
- there is a lot of learning in the subject
- you have to do the subject outside school
- it's difficult to get an A
- your brother told you it's really difficult
- there aren't many jobs available in that subject
- you think you might find the subject too difficult.

4 **Examine the remaining options** and decide what is best for you.

5 **Make your choice** and do what you need to do to carry it out. Have you decided what subjects you want to do? Then fill in the form.

6 **Review your decision.** Are you happy with your decision?

Group Work

In pairs think of some problem or decision from your own experience. Use the steps above to help you make the decision.

Pinpoint the decision

Smoke or   Not?

Identify your options

Smoke
Not.

List the advantages and disadvantages of each option

Advantages- "Look Cool", feel
confident.
Disadvantages- Lung failure

Examine the remaining options

I could die.

Make your choice

No I wont smoke

(Source: www.wsjclassroom.com)

From Conception to Birth

 ## Conception

After the female egg is fertilised by the male sperm it forms a single cell. This cell first divides into two, then into four, then into eight and so on. This ball of cells moves along the Fallopian tube to the womb. Once in the womb it divides into the embryo and placenta and embeds itself in the lining of the womb.

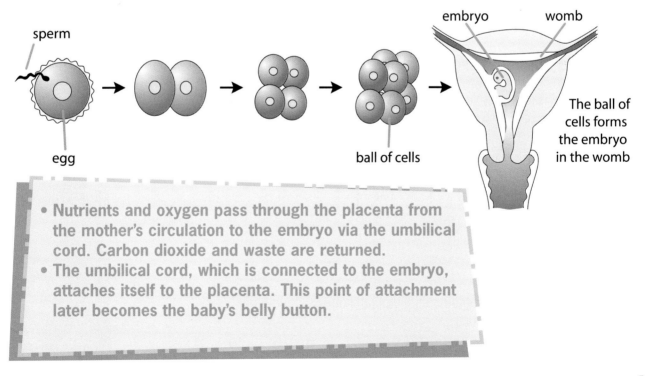

sperm

egg

ball of cells

embryo womb

The ball of cells forms the embryo in the womb

- Nutrients and oxygen pass through the placenta from the mother's circulation to the embryo via the umbilical cord. Carbon dioxide and waste are returned.
- The umbilical cord, which is connected to the embryo, attaches itself to the placenta. This point of attachment later becomes the baby's belly button.

→ Environment

- For the duration of the pregnancy the baby lives inside the uterus (womb).
- The baby is protected in a fluid-filled sac called the amniotic sac. This fluid is released during childbirth: this is what happens when the waters break.

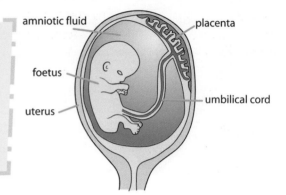

amniotic fluid

placenta

foetus

umbilical cord

uterus

→ Stages of Development

Week 8

At this stage the baby is referred to as a foetus rather than an embryo. All the baby's organs are in place and continue to develop. The face is forming, and if the mother were to have an ultrasound now, she would be able to hear the baby's heart beat. The arms and legs appear as buds. The baby is about the size of a five cent coin.

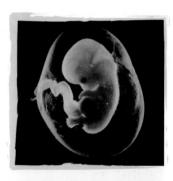

Week 12

Now the baby is fully formed and will continue to grow for the rest of the pregnancy. Features become more defined. Fingers and toes are fully formed. The placenta is fully developed, passing oxygen and nutrients from the mother to the baby and carrying carbon dioxide and waste away via the umbilical cord.

Week 18

By week eighteen eyelashes and eyebrows begin to grow. The mother will receive an ultrasound around this time. The ultrasound screens for any major defects, for example heart problems or spina bifida. The baby's sex can be identified at this stage. The baby will start to move. The baby's ears stand out and he/she will begin to hear in the coming weeks. The bones begin to harden. The baby is now about 11cm in length.

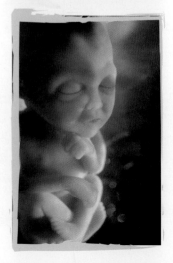

Week 28

The baby is now about the length of your forearm. The baby has reached a weight and stage of organ development that would enable it to survive outside the womb, though if it were born at this stage it would have to be kept in an incubator in a special neonatal unit. The baby would need help with breathing and feeding until it became more mature.

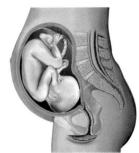

Week 36

The baby is more restricted within the uterus. The baby's head settles downwards in preparation for the birth.

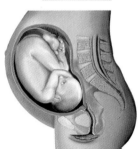

Weeks 37 – 40

The pregnancy has reached full term and the baby can be born at any time now. Its head is down waiting the birth. If the baby lies bottom down or feet first it is in the breech position.

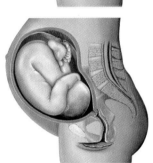

 **Birth**

There are three stages in the birth.
1 From the start of contractions to fully dilated.

- When the baby is ready to be born the mother experiences painful contractions. The contractions cause the neck of the womb to open. This allows the baby enough room to pass through. Over time, these contractions increase in strength and frequency.
- When the neck of the womb is fully dilated, or open, the baby is ready to be born. (Fully dilated is when the cervix is ten centimetres wide.)
- The waters can break at any time during childbirth.
- There are several different strategies to help the mother through labour pains. These include breathing/relaxation techniques, painkilling injections, an epidural, and entonox (gas and air).

2 From fully dilated to delivery of the baby.

- The baby moves through the birth canal (vagina), aided by the mother's pushing and the powerful contractions.
- When the widest part of the baby's head is delivered, this is known as crowning.
- Once the baby is delivered the umbilical cord is clamped and cut.
- The baby's first cry enables the lungs to inflate with air.

3 Delivery of the placenta.

- After the baby is born the placenta dislodges itself from the lining of the womb and is expelled by contractions.
- The mother sometimes receives an injection after the baby is born to aid this process.

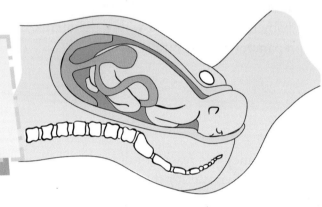

 # Caesarean Section

Caesarean section is when the baby is delivered by cutting the womb through the lower abdomen. This method is performed if there are complications in pregnancy or childbirth, for example breech birth, distressed baby, or if the cervix does not dilate fully.

 # A Healthy Pregnancy

- Anybody planning a baby should take folic acid before and during pregnancy up to the first fourteen weeks. Folic acid has been shown to reduce the risk of spina bifida.
- It is advised not to drink alcohol during pregnancy as it can affect the development of the growing foetus.
- Smoking during pregnancy causes lower birth weight babies.
- Drugs, e.g. cannabis, ecstasy and cocaine, may seriously harm the unborn baby.
- A pregnant woman should consult her GP before taking any medication.
- Certain foods eaten during pregnancy, such as unpasteurised dairy products, raw eggs and shellfish, could cause food poisoning and harm the unborn child and should be avoided.
- All pregnant woman are routinely tested for HIV during pregnancy. This is because if the test is positive certain drugs can be given to the mother to reduce the chances of the baby contracting the virus.

Sexual Reproduction Crossword

Across

8 This connects the embryo to the placenta and later forms the baby's belly button.

9 Food and oxygen pass from the mother to the baby through this.

10 This occurs when the widest part of the baby's head is delivered.

11 These occur when the baby is ready to be born.

12 The joining together of the female's egg and the male's sperm.

Down

1 _____ dairy products should be avoided during pregnancy.

2 You should take this if you are planning to have a baby.

3 The egg is located here when it is ready to be fertilised.

4 This fluid protects the baby and prevents it being injured.

5 A normal pregnancy lasts about _____ months.

6 This waste substance passes from the baby to the mother.

7 The baby lives here for the duration of the pregnancy.

Label the diagram below:

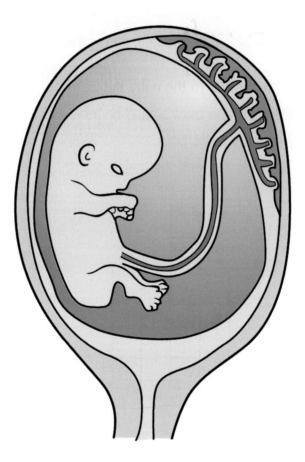

Describe the development of the baby at each stage below:

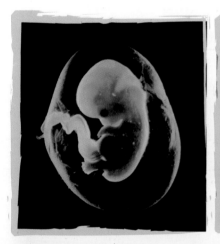 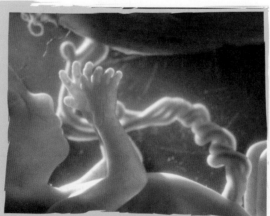 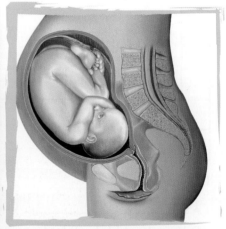

 Useful Websites

www.justthefacts.ie
www.mindbodyandsoul.gov.uk
www.lifebytes.gov.uk
www.kidshealth.org

Recognising and Expressing Feelings and Emotions

In first year you learned about the importance of expressing how you feel. Recap below why it is important to show how you feel.

_____

_____

_____

Sometimes people write songs to help them express how they feel. In pairs, read the words of the following song or listen to it. Answer the questions that follow. Discuss your answers as a class.

Chasing Cars
(Snow Patrol)

We'll do it all
Everything
On our own

We don't need
Anything
Or anyone

If I lay here
If I just lay here
Would you lie with me and just forget the world?

I don't quite know
How to say
How I feel

Those three words
Are said too much
They're not enough

If I lay here
If I just lay here
Would you lie with me and just forget the world?

Forget what we're told
Before we get too old
Show me a garden that's bursting into life

Let's waste time
Chasing cars
Around our heads

I need your grace
To remind me
To find my own

If I lay here
If I just lay here
Would you lie with me and
just forget the world?

Forget what we're told
Before we get too old
Show me a garden that's
bursting into life

All that I am
All that I ever was
Is here in your perfect
eyes, they're all I can see
I don't know where

Confused about how as well
Just know that these things
will never change for us at all

If I lay here
If I just lay here
Would you lie with me and just
forget the world?

What do you think the song is about?

_____

_____

_____

How do you think the person in the song feels?

_____

_____

_____

Do you think a song is a good way of expressing your emotions? In what other ways do people express their emotions?

_____

_____

_____

Do you think boys and girls differ in the way they show their emotions?

_____

_____

_____

Do you think it is normal and acceptable to have high and low emotions?

_____

_____

_____

When you are a teenager you may notice changes in your mood. At times you feel in great form and at times you feel really fed up. A child expresses their feelings freely, they can show their affection with a hug, or if they are annoyed they might sulk or have a tantrum. As we grow older we are expected to recognise our feelings and express them in a controlled way.

As you learned in first year, holding our feelings inside and not expressing them only leads to stress in the long run. At the same time we cannot just lash out at a person if we get annoyed. The important thing is to learn to deal with your feelings and express them in an appropriate way.

Below is a list of feelings. Sort them into two columns: those that society deems it is acceptable to show; and those society deems it is not OK to show.

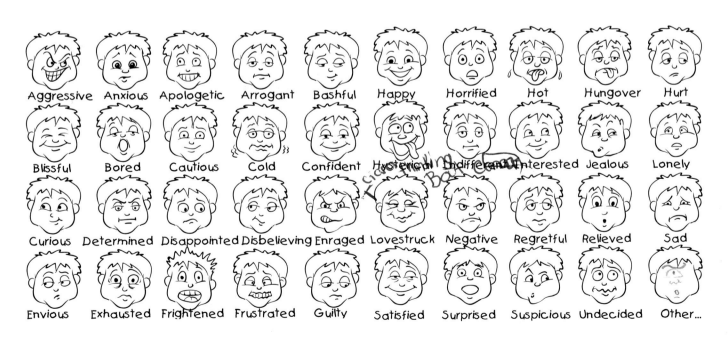

| Aggressive | Anxious | Apologetic | Arrogant | Bashful | Happy | Horrified | Hot | Hungover | Hurt |

| Blissful | Bored | Cautious | Cold | Confident | Hysterical | Indifferent | Interested | Jealous | Lonely |

| Curious | Determined | Disappointed | Disbelieving | Enraged | Lovestruck | Negative | Regretful | Relieved | Sad |

| Envious | Exhausted | Frightened | Frustrated | Guilty | Satisfied | Surprised | Suspicious | Undecided | Other... |

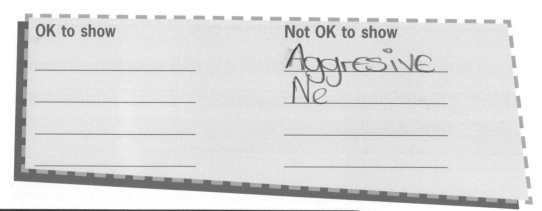

OK to show	Not OK to show
_____	Aggresive
_____	Ne _____
_____	_____
_____	_____

Class Activity

Why do you think it is OK to show some feelings and not others?

When you were a child you were totally dependent on your parents to look after you and to make decisions for you. Now, at adolescence, you have more responsibilities and you have to consider your own feelings and the feelings of others. At this stage this is all pretty new, so you have to learn to recognise your feelings and express them appropriately.

 # Learning to Get Along

In every relationship people will have their disagreements. The important thing is that these disagreements do not get out of control. You do not want disagreements to turn into a screaming match or people throwing accusations at each other. There can be a lot of reasons for rifts and disagreements but it is important that people try to discuss their feelings in a way that allows an agreement to be reached.

Can you identify some of the possible rifts or disagreements between the following people?

A teenager and their family	Friends	Boyfriend/girlfriend

Group Work

Read the following scenarios. What seems to be the issue?

How do you think it could be resolved in each case?

Denise and Emma

Denise has fancied Paul for as long as she can remember. Recently Denise went on holidays to Spain. On returning home she found out that her best friend Emma has started seeing Paul. She is meeting Emma tonight.

Conor

Conor has been seeing Lucy for about two months. At the beginning she always hung out with him and his friends. Lately, however, she seems reluctant to meet him when he is with his friends. So if he wants to spend time with her, it means he is spending less time with his friends and more time with hers. His friends are starting to give him a hard time, telling him he is a lap dog and that he is under the thumb. Conor really likes Lucy but he is growing sick of the slagging. What should he do?

In order to resolve problems in a relationship it is very important to be able to express how you feel without the situation getting worse. The best way to resolve issues in a relationship is to:

- try to sort out the problem as soon as possible
- wait until the person is calm to talk to them
- do not bring up past disagreements
- explain to the other person that something is bothering you and you want to talk about it
- say how you feel – calmly, without raising your voice
- give the other person a chance to respond and say how they feel
- tell the person exactly what they are doing that is bothering you – do not insult them
- tell them how the problem is affecting you
- try to reach an agreement that is best for both of you.

Using these guidelines, role play the scenarios above.

Managing Relationships

 Boyfriend / Girlfriend Relationships

When you are ready to start a relationship with a boy or a girl it is very important that you do so for the right reasons. Be your own person, do what feels right for you. Just because some of your friends are in a relationship does not mean you have to follow suit. People do not have to be in a relationship to prove something. There may be other things in your life that are far more important to you at the moment, for example friends, sport, study. Just because you are not interested in anyone at the moment does not mean you won't be in the future – your time will come.

When you are ready to be in a relationship it is very important to be able to recognise the qualities that make a good relationship. Choose the five qualities you think are most important from the list below.

honest ✓
trustworthy ✓
good looking ✓
intelligent
similar interests
nice clothes
nice hair

funny ✓
sense of humour
caring
respect for others
loyal
there for you

spends all their time with you
can share how you feel with them
wealthy
fun to be with ✓
generous

Group Work

In groups discuss the following questions and write down the answers you come up with.

Do you think it is important to have a boyfriend or girlfriend at your age? Why?

live yeh life
They hold you Back

Give reasons why someone of your age may choose to have a boyfriend or girlfriend.

Want to be cool.

May like the lad.

Faith, Blind date.

Give reasons why someone of your age may not choose to have a boyfriend or girlfriend.

Lesbian,

Class Discussion

What sort of boy/girl relationships do your parents accept at the moment?

Do you agree with their opinion? Do you find it easy to talk to your parents about girlfriends and boyfriends?

 # Peer Pressure and Other Influences

Who are your peers? Your peers are people of similar age to you, who share many of the same interests as you. Have you ever stopped to think how much you are influenced what your friends do and say? Probably not!

Peer pressure can be positive or negative. It's positive when someone pressurises you into doing something that is good for you or someone else; and negative when it is something that will be bad for you or for someone else.

Group Work

Below are some examples of positive and negative peer pressure. Can you add more examples?

Positive	Negative
Encouraging a friend to train hard to get on the team	Encouraging you to damage property
_____	_____
_____	_____
_____	_____

Sometimes it is hard to pinpoint peer pressure, but it is there and it affects all people at different ages and in different walks of life. Answer the following questions to find out how influential peer pressure is in your life. Tick the appropriate box: Like Me or Not Like Me.

1. **You go along with your friends even if you do not agree with what they are doing.**
   Like me ☐
   Not like me ☐
2. **It is important for you that you do not stand out from your peers.**
   Like me ☐
   Not like me ☐
3. **You would go along with your friends just so you do not lose face.**
   Like me ☐
   Not like me ☐
4. **You feel embarrassed if you are not allowed do what your friends are doing.**
   Like me ☐
   Not like me ☐
5. **You find it difficult to stand up for what you believe in at times.**
   Like me ☐
   Not like me ☐

Teenagers are probably the people who are most influenced by peer pressure. Have you ever been pressurised to do something because you were worried you would be different if you didn't? Emotionally you are trying to find your own feet, so you look for reassurance from others.

Standing up to peer pressure can be difficult. Most people want to fit in and to be liked, so sometimes we go along with the crowd so as not to be left out. Peer pressure to dress a certain way is one thing, but going along with the crowd to drink and smoke is another.

Class Discussion

Do you believe that peer pressure is an issue for young people?

Discuss the more serious implications of peer pressure.

 # How to Resist Peer Pressure

There can be a lot of pressure on young teenagers to get involved in stuff that they really do not want to do. The important thing is to stand up for what you believe in. Sometimes it's not as easy as just saying no: even when you say no the person hassling you won't always back down or walk away. Resisting peer pressure means you recognise what is important to you in your life and with this in mind you decide what you will never do no matter what!

Below make a list of things you will never do no matter what. Examples might be taking drugs, stealing, having underage sex.

_____

_____

_____

Tips on Resisting Peer Pressure

Now that you know what you will never do, how do you stand up to peer pressure? Peer pressure can range from gentle persuasion to intimidation. Here are some helpful tips:

- It's your life – you do not have to give anyone any excuses for what you believe in.
- Decide what you want to say and stick to it.
- When you say no, say it clearly.
- Do not be persuaded by others making you feel guilty or saying things like, 'If you were my friend you'd do it.'
- Do not fight back or make accusations.
- A true friend will respect your decision no matter what. They will not fall out with you simply because you do not want to do something.
- If the pressure does not stop walk away.

Role Play

Resisting the pressure to drink

Role play the following situation.

You are on a school trip in France when one of your friends takes a bottle of coke containing vodka from her bag. She drinks some of the vodka then your other friend takes a drink. Then they both try to persuade you to drink. They are very persistent.

Characters: two people will be doing the persuading. One person will try to resist. Each person must take turns at each role.

How did you feel about being pressured?

_____

_____

How did you feel about pressurising others?

_____

_____

_____

Was it easier to have someone join you?

_____

_____

_____

Why do you think people pressure other people into making decisions?

_____

_____

_____

Write about a time you experienced peer pressure. What was said on this occasion?

Would you do anything differently if it happened now?

_____

_____

_____

_____

Class Discussion

A group of students in your class have been giving a new teacher a hard time. You, along with a few more students, are concerned that you are not getting the course covered.

What would you like to do in this situation?

What could you do?

Case Study

Pamela has been going out with John for a couple of months now. Valerie is a very good friend of Pamela's but lately she feels like a bit of a gooseberry. Pamela is constantly trying to set Valerie up with John's friend Kevin. Pamela has met Kevin and likes him but she does not feel ready to start dating him. Pamela has told Valerie that the next time they meet up she will leave them on their own together. Valerie does not want that.

Questions for Discussion

What should Valerie do?

Do you think Pamela is being fair to her friend?

Should Valerie meet Kevin and just see what happens?

 Useful Website

www.mindbodyandsoul.gov.uk/emotional

Making Responsible Decisions

Remember: when making a decision, you should not be bullied into anything that goes against your personal values or that you will regret later. It is important to respect yourself and others; you must consider your own health and safety at all times.

What to you think are important values in a relationship?

_____

_____

_____

_____

What are the consequences, both emotional and physical, of underage sex?

_____

_____

_____

Group Work

In each of the following situations:

- **pinpoint** the decision to be made
- **identify** the options available
- **list** the advantages and disadvantages of each option, and consider what's important to you
- **examine** the remaining options
- **make your choice** and take steps to carry it out.

Sarah has been going out with John for a couple of months. She fancied him for ages. He was so popular and good looking that she could not believe it when he started to take an interest in her. It was great at the start. She felt she was the envy of all her classmates and it felt good to be seen with him. Lately John has started to make subtle remarks about her appearance that upset her. Sometimes he lets her down and does not show up when he says he will. He often gets in a bad mood and takes it out on her. Sarah feels that this will change and that things will be good again. She really likes him and does not feel that she will meet anyone else, let alone someone as good looking as John.

- **pinpoint** the decision to be made

Break up with him or Not

- **identify** the options available

Dump him & keep your dignity.

- **list** the advantages and disadvantages of each option, and consider what's important to you

Don①:

- **examine** the remaining options

- **make your choice** and take steps to carry it out.

- *pinpoint* the decision to be made

_____

_____

- *identify* the options available

_____

_____

- *list* the advantages and disadvantages of each option, and consider what's important to you

_____

_____

- *examine* the remaining options

_____

_____

- *make your choice* and take steps to carry it out.

_____

_____

Emily has been seeing Cian for over two months now. They get on really well together. Just last week Cian told Emily that his parents are away for the weekend, so he has a free house. He asked her to stay over Saturday night. Emily really likes Cian but she is not ready for this. She is worried, however, that if she does not go Cian will not understand. She does not want to lose him.

Health and Safety

Group Work

In first year you looked at important guidelines on how to protect yourself and keep yourself safe. Working in groups, recap these guidelines.

_____

_____

_____

When starting a new relationship you must use your common sense. Do not take any risks until you know the person well and you can trust them. Although you may feel they are trustworthy you can never be too careful. Some people can take advantage of your naivety, so be aware at all times. You can never be too careful.

Module 8

Emotional Health

 ## Self-confidence and Self-esteem

What does it mean to be self-confident?

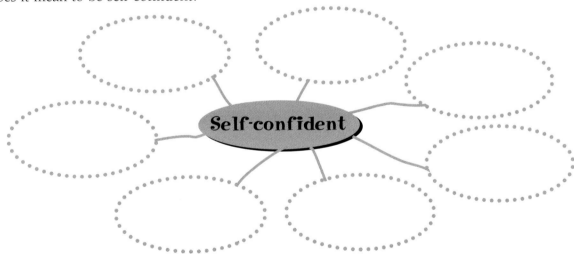

Self-confident

Having confidence is sometimes seen as a bad thing. You may have heard people say, 'He loves himself,' or 'she thinks she's it.' Being confident is not about being boastful or overpowering. It's about recognising your own strengths and being happy with who you are as a person. Self-respect and respect for others helps you to become more confident. Below write down ten things you are good at, or ten good things you have done, or a combination of both.

(For example: I have a good sense of humour; I am kind to an elderly neighbour; I am good at playing the piano.)

_____

_____

_____

_____

Class Discussion

Was it difficult to make this list?

Why do you think we are sometimes afraid to tell people about the good things we have done?

Even though we can recognise others' strengths, we can be our own worst critics. Some people have poor self-esteem and put themselves down; this can result in a person not achieving all they can. If you believe in yourself you can be the best you possibly can. Having positive self-esteem is closely linked to having good self-confidence. Listed below are examples of positive self-esteem and negative self-esteem. Can you add to this list?

Positive self-esteem	Negative self-esteem
Can stand up for yourself	Putting yourself down
Happy with the way you look	Worried about what others think

The Average Child
by Mike Buscemi

I don't cause teachers trouble;
My grades have been okay.
I listen in my classes.
I'm in school every day.
My teachers think I'm average;
My parents think so too.
I wish I didn't know that, though;
There's lots I'd like to do.
I'd like to build a rocket;
I read a book on how.

Or start a stamp collection ...
But no use trying now.
'Cause, since I found I'm average,
I'm smart enough you see
To know there's nothing special
I should expect of me.
I'm part of that majority,
That hump part of the bell,
Who spends his life unnoticed
In an average kind of hell.

Class Discussion

1 How do you think the child in this poem feels?

2 What influences how he feels about himself?

3 He speaks about being unnoticed; did you ever feel like this?

 # Criticism

We have all been criticised at some stage in our lives. Sometimes we may feel hard done by or victimised. We might want to dismiss or reject the criticism we hear. It is important to realise that not all criticism is bad. It may be something we need to hear and it is for our benefit. For example, your coach tells you that you need to work on your weak side in hurling; or your teacher tells you that you have to start getting your essays in on time. This criticism may be valid – perhaps you always hand in your essays late. This type of criticism is called constructive criticism. The person giving it only wants to help you. The teacher is simply trying to make you more organised and meet deadlines. Your coach wants you to improve your skill level to become a better player. You have to decide whether the criticism is deserved or not. If you know the criticism is valid than you need to accept that and try to do something about it.

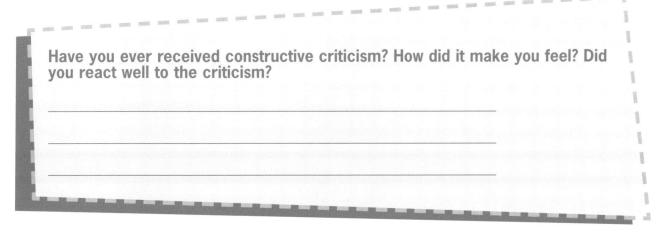

Have you ever received constructive criticism? How did it make you feel? Did you react well to the criticism?

_____

_____

_____

Some of the criticism we receive is undeserved. You may be unjustly compared to a sister or brother on your performance in school. This may affect your self-esteem. Sometimes you may be criticised and it's not your fault. For example, you get a detention for not having done your homework even though a family problem prevented you from getting it done. This type of criticism is hard to take as you may get annoyed at being wronged. Again, try to decide whether you deserve the criticism or not. Use assertive communication. Try to explain yourself calmly: it may or may not make a difference, but it's better than saying nothing.

Have you ever been unfairly criticised? How did you react?

_____

_____

_____

The third type of criticism is purely spiteful and its only aim is to insult or upset the person, for example if a person slags your clothes or your appearance. Everyone has something they are self-conscious about, and receiving an insult about that particular thing can really get to you. The important thing is not to dwell on the criticism. Do not take it personally and definitely do not believe it.

Individual Work

Have you ever been in a situation where someone said something that made you feel bad about yourself? How did it make you feel?

_____

_____

_____

Group Work

Come up with some ways of handling destructive criticism.

_____

_____

_____

Think Positive Thoughts

One way to learn to become more confident is to talk positively to ourselves. When we put ourselves down we can start to believe that what we say is true, and this can directly affect our self-esteem. This is sometimes called 'negative self-talk' or 'killer talk'.

To gain self-confidence it is important to replace negative self-talk with positive self-talk.

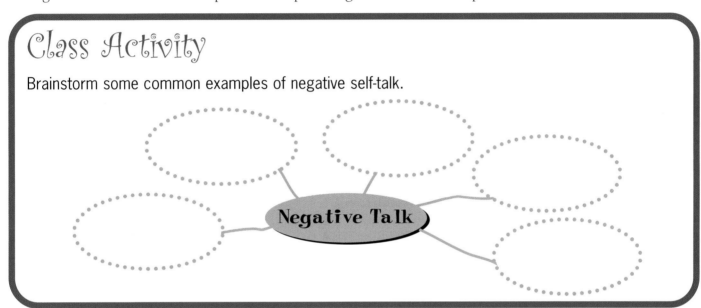

Class Activity

Brainstorm some common examples of negative self-talk.

Negative Talk

In each of the situations below change the negative talk to positive talk.
One has been done for you.

1 You fail a history exam

Negative talk: 'I am useless at this subject.'

Positive talk: 'Next time I'm really going to work harder and do better.'

2 You find out a group of your friends went to the cinema without asking you.

Negative talk: 'Maybe I'm just not fun to be around.'

Positive talk: _____

3 You meet a boy/girl from school, you go bright red and you are stuck for something to say.

Negative talk: 'I made such a fool of myself.'

Positive talk: _____

4 You're studying for an exam.

Negative talk: 'I'm so stupid I'll never pass the exam.'

Positive talk: _____

Individual Work

Write down some of the negative talk you say about yourself and convert it to positive talk.

Negative talk	Positive Talk

Weekly Task

Try to practise positive self-talk for the coming week.

 # Body Image and Self-esteem

Write down your image of an ideal girl and an ideal boy below. Use the headings to help you.

	Ideal Boy	Ideal Girl
Qualities		
Physical features		
Personality		

Class Discussion

Compare your results. Do you think that such an ideal boy or girl exists?

Where do you think these ideals come from?

Body image is the mental picture a person has of their own body. Are you happy with your body? No matter who you ask, very few people will answer 'yes' to this question. Everyone has something they are not happy with.

Having a positive body image as a teenager is difficult because your body is changing and developing. And it is made all the more difficult when the media bombard us with images of 'beautiful', flawless people.

If we were to go by the media, the ideal image for a girl is to be thin and for a boy it is to be strong and muscular. But these images are unrealistic: most people do not match this ideal. It is only natural to want to look good, but when we compare ourselves to these 'ideal' images we can concentrate on appearance alone and lose sight of all the other qualities we have. As the saying goes, 'Beauty is only skin deep.'

The media's obsession with looks and weight overlooks the fact that people are different and we all have different shapes and sizes. In the past the ideal woman was a large woman – this was seen as a sign of wealth – but in the 1960s the waif-like model figure became the ideal. Not fitting the ideal does not mean a person is not beautiful.

Read the following article.

It took 4 experts 3 days to get our model looking like this ...

Before ▼

After ▲

Next time you flick through a magazine and feel bad for not matching up to the flawless images that bombard you – stop, it's not that easy. **Roxanne Parker** *reports.*

Working as a fashion stylist I've learnt that physical perfection is an illusion created by a team of professionals who pool their talents to make a model look terrific.

Most of us who pick flaws in our appearance have only seen snapshots of ourselves. Yet we are comparing ourselves to retouched professional and celebrity photos that have taken days and big budgets to create.

'I won't know who the model is when I arrive on a job, and I've often make the mistake of thinking the model is a member of the crew,' says leading make-up artist Zoe Clark.

For this shoot, Zoe, Liam Boland, artistic director of Toni & Guy Belfast, photographer Jim Fitzpatrick and myself as stylist worked together for ten hours to achieve [a selection of shots] of professional model Ruth Scallon. Before the shoot started, I spent a day sourcing clothes and another day returning them. Jim spent two days sorting, editing and retouching the final selection of photos.

Even when working with a natural beauty like Ruth, it still

takes a huge amount of work to transform a model into the super-beauty we have grown accustomed to seeing in magazines. Here, our team disclose their secrets.

The Model

'I think most models arrive at a job feeling embarrassed as you come with no make-up on. I always feel that the hair and make-up crew must be thinking, "is that what we have to work with?"

'But it's a model's job to be a blank canvas so your own look can be adapted to whatever the job requires. Sometimes it's difficult to recognise yourself in photos as your image can be changed so drastically.

'Recently, my father didn't recognise me in a shot. I asked him if I was in the paper that day and he said no – yet my photo was on the front page of the *Irish Independent* in his hand!'

The Make-up Artist

'No model or celebrity arrives looking flawless. They all have spots and dark circles that need covering,' says Zoe.

'Irish magazines regularly fly models in from Prague or London for shoots. The girls arrive exhausted, having caught a flight at 3.30am for the shoot. It's my job to make them look awake.

'I'll apply a soothing face mask, cooling eye gel, eye drops, and use an ivory pencil on the inside of their eyes to take the red out – and that's before I start on the make-up.'

On other jobs Zoe has had to conceal cold sores, wipe noses, pluck bikini lines and other extremes.

'I once had to apply lipstick to a model's nipples because the stylist didn't think they looked pink enough!'

Not to mention the sunburned, peeling model who had applied a fake tan the night before a job.

'She looked like a burns victim! I had to get her into a shower to scrub her skin, then I covered her in Elizabeth Arden Eight Hour Cream mixed with body lotion before coating her in concealer!'

For Ruth's photos, Zoe used fake eyelashes and liquid eyeliner to change the shape of Ruth's eyes and make them look bigger.

'I sculpted Ruth's cheekbones using a contouring colour – this gave her better bone structure. It took one hour to complete the look, plus constant retouching, including body make-up and foundation for hands to stop them looking cold.'

The Photographer

Jim says: 'When I started digital photography seven years ago I used a lot of retouching. With one of Ireland's leading models, I lengthened her legs, slimmed her waist and enhanced her flesh tones using Photoshop for her portfolio shots. Back then, it was a novelty to retouch. Now I refuse to augment a girl's body with retouching. I'll fix spots and fly-away hairs, but that's it.

'I firmly believe that photo manipulation can be as dangerous to the female psyche as the cult of size zero or the "heroin chic" look.

'Too much Photoshop looks ridiculous. Remember Kate Winslet on the cover of *GQ*? They did so much Photoshop to her body she was hardly recognisable. These days, even very young girls have impossible body images spread in front of them in teen magazines.

'Ruth's shots took two days to work on. Most of this time was spent sorting through the 1,000 images to find the best shots. After that, I cleaned them up and adjusted the light balance.'

The Hairdresser

Liam says, 'Models' hair can be in poor condition due to the amount of styling and blow-drying they endure. I use products to disguise this wear and tear.

'Serum temporarily seals split ends, while thickening sprays bulk out flat hair. For this shoot the brief was long, Swinging Sixties hair. Ruth's hair is neck-length naturally, so I had to use €200 worth of real human hair to extend the length.

'The hair comes in strips called wefts, which I unroll and cut to size. They are glued to the scalp and last two to three weeks. Hair for shoots needs to be three times larger than real life or else it gets lost in photos. It took two hours to get Ruth's hair right.'

Liam knows that even celebrities have bad hair days, as proved when working on a famous American actress's hair for the cover of a magazine. The young brunette, who made her name starring in teen horror films, arrived at the shoot with her hair extensions falling out!

'She had them put in for her last movie but they were falling out, so I had to use headscarves and clever up-styles to conceal the bald patches.'

So there you have it. The next time you look through a magazine and feel bad about yourself, keep in mind that if you had a team of professionals grooming you you'd look pretty good too.

(Source: Irish Independent 17 April 2007)

Class Discussion

Do you think the media put pressure on young people to look a certain way?

Can it affect your opinion of yourself and others?

 ## Useful Website

www.bodywhys.ie

 # Your Body

There are certain features of our bodies that we can change. It is important to identify these and, if necessary, to go about changing them in a healthy and safe way. From the list below, choose with elements you can change and which you cannot.

height	weight	muscle	mouth
hair	posture	size	nose
eyes	ears	feet	level of fitness
bone structure	teeth	complexion	hands

What you can change

_____
_____
_____

What you cannot change

_____
_____
_____

→ Body Types

Your body type is largely determined by heredity. Body types can be classified into three main types: endomorph; ectomorph; and mesomorph. A person seldom fits exactly one type: normally a person's body type leans more towards one type than another.

- *Endomorphs* tend to have round body types, with more body fat and softer curves, wider hips, large abdomen, shorter legs.
- *Ectomorphs* tend to be thin, with small bones, slender arms and legs, less curvy, more angular.
- *Mesomorphs* tend to be more muscular, with wide shoulders and slim hips, powerful legs and broad shoulders.

Can you identify each person's body type in the pictures above?

Tips for Improving Your Body Image

Some people feel that if only they could change the way they look they would be happy. It is more important to be happy with yourself as you are. Improving your self-esteem is a vital part of improving your own body image. Remember: everyone is unhappy with some aspect of themselves but no one is perfect. Living your life being envious of others is not the answer. Be realistic about your own shape.

If there are things you want to change (such as getting fitter or losing weight), set yourself a goal, for example to eat healthily and exercise every day.

Have you ever bought new clothes that make you feel really good about yourself when you wear them? Dressing to suit your shape can also boost your body image. Wear clothes that complement your good points.

- *Concentrate on the good things about yourself.*
- *Write a list of positive things about yourself and add to it often.*
- *Spend time with people who are positive and supportive and make you feel good about yourself.*

Module 9

Substance Abuse

 ## The Effects of Drugs

A drug is any substance that alters the way the body acts or feels. In first year you learned about the benefits of drugs. Unfortunately there are some people who choose to abuse their body by using drugs. Drug abuse can involve legal or illegal drugs. It can be:

- *physical* – when it damages a person's health
- *mental* or *emotional* – there is a change in the person's behaviour
- *social* – it harms a person's relationships.

Using the spider diagram below, try to brainstorm the different ways drug abuse can damage aspects of a person's life.

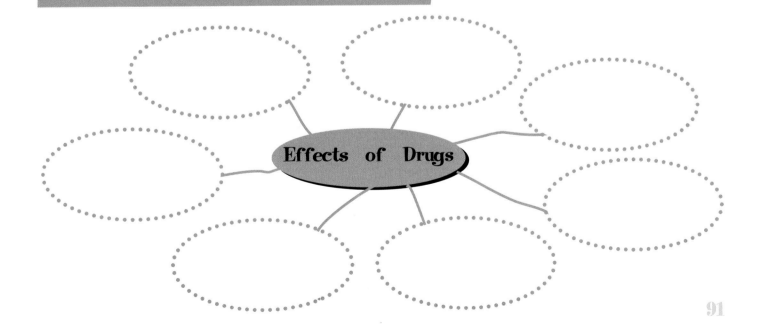

Effects of Drugs

Taking Drugs

Different illegal drugs cause harm in different ways. Drugs can be taken by mouth, inhaled, injected or sniffed. The drug is absorbed into the bloodstream and carried to the brain. Drugs that are injected are generally thought to be more dangerous because of the risks involved in sharing needles. Each drug, however, carries its own risks.

 # Types of Drugs

There are five main drug types.

- *Depressants (downers)* such as alcohol calm the mind and cause sleepiness.
- *Sedatives and tranquillisers* such as Valium calm people down and can be addictive.
- *Opiates* such as heroin cause a feeling of happiness.
- *Stimulants (uppers)* such as cocaine and ecstasy make people feel more energetic.
- *Hallucinogens* such as LSD, magic mushrooms and cannabis distort the way you see or hear things.

 # Addiction/Dependence

In groups, try to come up with a definition of addiction.

_____

_____

_____

What might people become addicted to?

_____

_____

_____

Drug Addiction

When we think of the word addiction we probably think of the smoker who smokes forty cigarettes a day and proclaims they cannot give them up. An addiction means that a person is dependent on a drug and feels they are unable to cope without it. Some addictions are more dangerous than others, depending on the drug and the extent to which the person depends on the drug.

People who start taking drugs believe they will not become dependent or addicted. This is not always the case. For some drugs, if your body builds up a tolerance for a drug you need more of it each time to gain the same effect. There are two types of addiction: physical and psychological.

Physical Addiction

In this case the absence of the drug in the user's body can cause withdrawal symptoms. The person has to be weaned off the drug to overcome their physical addiction. Withdrawal symptoms can include vomiting, sweating, shakes, muscular pain, cramps, constipation.

Psychological Addiction

This is when the user feels they need the drug to be happy, feel normal or to cope with life.
(Source: 'Drugs: There are Answers', Health Promotion Unit)

Read the following story, then answer the questions that follow.

The Story of an Addict

I grew up in a decent family; I had good parents, played sports, got average grades, and had good friends. I began drinking in secondary school, occasionally I smoked cannabis. I never felt there was a problem as all my friends did it too. Then I went away to college and I started to smoke a lot more cannabis and I justified this by telling myself, 'I'm only experimenting'. I started to do less work at college as I would spend most evenings smoking cannabis with friends. What I found also was that when I started to use cannabis the opportunity to use other drugs arose. I kept telling myself I was only experimenting, so when the opportunity arose to take some cocaine I took it. I was interested in knowing what type of high the drug would give me.

I was at a friend's house one night smoking some cannabis and a guy showed up with some heroin. So, having the mentality that I was only experimenting, I thought I would give it a go. I snorted heroin that night for the first time. I enjoyed using it but I did not feel that I could get addicted at this point. I could quit this at any stage. The more heroin I used the more I felt I needed to get the same high. I then decided I would start injecting. I thought I would try this and it shouldn't have any effect on my school, family, or life as a whole. But I was wrong. After that first shot of heroin, it gave me that false euphoric feeling I had never known before; *it became my girlfriend, my God, my mother and my career.*

For the next few years, I shot heroin every single day Eventually, I had to drop out of college because the heroin habit consumed 100 per cent of my time. I ultimately had to move back into my mother's house. Right before moving back home, I spent twenty-five grand in four months, all on heroin. Not because I wanted to, but my habit had got so large, I thought I had to. This damn powder and needle had its grip on me so tight that I needed to stick a syringe in my arm numerous times throughout the day just to function and to feel normal. It was extremely sick and twisted.

I had to find other ways to support this devilish habit. I began by driving friends around to bulk stores and supermarkets to steal, and eventually I joined in. This led to breaking into innocent people's homes to steal cash, I stole from my family. I hated myself but I would do anything to feed my habit.

(Anonymous, adapted from 'An Addict's Story', www.heroinabuse.net)

Class Discussion

1. Why did he start taking drugs?

2. How do you think his story will end (a) if he stops his habit and (b) if he continues his habit?

3. What do think caused him to change the drugs he was taking?

4. At what point would you say he had become addicted?

Group Work

Despite the risks some young people continue to take drugs. Below are some reasons why young people take drugs. Can you add some more reasons?

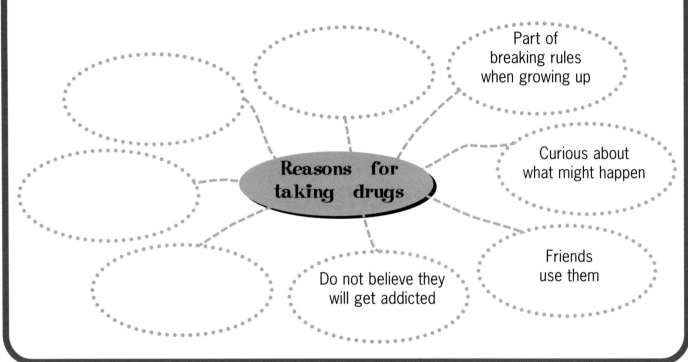

Reasons for taking drugs

Part of breaking rules when growing up

Curious about what might happen

Friends use them

Do not believe they will get addicted

Drugs Quiz

How much do you remember?

1 A hallucinogen is a drug that:

    a) changes the way you see or hear things

    b) increases energy levels

    c) eases pain.

2 An example of a stimulant is:

    a) cannabis

    b) Valium

    c) ecstasy.

4 Alcohol is:

    a) a depressant

    b) a stimulant

    c) not a drug.

3 If your body builds up a tolerance for a drug it means:

    a) the drug has no effect on you

    b) you need more of the drug to achieve the same effect

    c) you can no longer take the drug.

 # Cannabis and its Effects

Answer the following quiz to find out how much you know about cannabis:

Cannabis Quiz:

	True	False
1 Cannabis is the most commonly used illegal drug.	❏	❏
2 Cannabis is legal in Ireland.	❏	❏
3 Cannabis is a stimulant.	❏	❏
4 Smoking cannabis can cause panic, anxiety or confusion.	❏	❏
5 People who use cannabis are not likely to use other drugs.	❏	❏
6 Smoking joints carries a greater risk of cancer than smoking cigarettes.	❏	❏
7 Grass is a form of cannabis.	❏	❏
8 You cannot get addicted to cannabis.	❏	❏
9 You can be arrested if you are found smoking cannabis in public.	❏	❏
10 The maximum penalty for possession of cannabis is three years' imprisonment.	❏	❏
11 Cannabis can be detected in your system a month after use.	❏	❏

Soloutions:

1 T, 2 F, 3 F, 4 T, 5 F, 6 T, 7 T, 8 F, 9 T, 10 T, 11 T.

Cannabis and its Effects

→ What is Cannabis?

Cannabis comes in three forms:

- *grass* – looks like dried herbs
- *resin* – looks like an Oxo cube; it is scraped down for use
- *oil* – the strongest form; rarely seen in Ireland.

Slang names for cannabis include hash, blow, dope, grass, weed.

Cannabis is usually smoked with tobacco in a joint or a spliff. It is one of the most commonly used of all illegal drugs, and it can stay in your system for up to forty days, depending on how often you use it and how much you use.

The effects of cannabis can last for several hours, depending on the amount used and the strength of the cannabis.

Cannabis can:

1 cause sensations of fearfulness, anxiety or confusion

2 produce more tar than smoking cigarettes, so there can be a greater risk of cancer

3 affect short-term memory, concentration and motivation

4 develop psychological dependence, with sustained use

5 increase a person's chances of being offered or using other drugs.

(*Source: www.mqi.ie*)

Answer the following questions.

What are the three forms of cannabis?

1_____

2_____

3_____

List three risks of smoking cannabis

1_____

2_____

3_____

How long can cannabis stay in a person's system?

_____

Cannabis: Why/Why Not?

Brainstorm why you think people use cannabis.

Why use cannabis?

A lot of people have no interest in taking drugs. Sometimes people start taking drugs simply because an opportunity arises. People may feel awkward or embarrassed about saying no. Read the story below and discuss the questions that follow.

Have a go!

Kate's parents are away so she has asked Jean and a few more friends from school over to her house. Kate's boyfriend Martin is there. Jean knows that Martin smokes cannabis, and Kate has started to smoke it quite a bit since they started going out together. Jean has often been in their company when they smoke, but when the joint is passed around she always refuses. As they are chatting Martin starts to roll a joint. Jean knows that as soon as he lights up, she will be offered a drag. Tonight she feels if she says no again, she will look like an idiot and that the whole school will know about it. She really has no interest but everyone is trying it. Kate keeps telling her it's no big deal and it's not one of the dangerous drugs.

Class Discussion

Do you think this story is realistic?

What should Jean do if she does not wish to smoke cannabis?

Is her friend being fair to her?

Where would you be most likely to be offered cannabis?

Remember – you have the right to say no. You won't look stupid if you refuse. Use some of the assertiveness skills you learned in Chapter 3.

Alcohol and its Effects

Group Work

Read the following comments. Do you agree with the teenagers' opinions? Give a reason for your answer in each case and discuss your answers with the class.

'There is no point in telling young people about the dangers of drinking, they will do it anyway. Peer pressure has a big impact on their drinking habits.'

_____

_____

_____

'Getting drunk every week is stupid, but having a couple of drinks is OK.'

_____

_____

_____

'The legal age for drinking should be reduced to 16.'

_____

_____

_____

'You're not harming anybody by underage drinking.'

_____

_____

_____

'There is nothing to do in our area, so people drink in groups to pass the time.'

_____

_____

_____

'There's no point in drinking unless you get drunk.'

_____

_____

_____

'If you don't drink you should not be pressurised into it.'

_____

_____

_____

Alcohol: Why/Why Not?

Group Work

Read the following article and discuss the questions that follow, first in groups, then as a class.

Faced with the sober reality of a drunken night out with our teens

We're no longer shocked by images of intoxicated teens, but we should realise that they're putting their lives in danger, says **Emma Blain**

As the commuters queued for the buses to go home, the teenagers began to queue to get into the nightclubs around town. At half past six on a busy city street, the barriers went up outside one of the clubs to keep order among the youngsters who were celebrating the results of their Junior Cert.

First in line are the boys, with their spiked-up hair and pastel-coloured T-shirts, then they are joined by their girlfriends, who are whooping and shouting with joy at the results they received earlier on in the day. After a few minutes, a small boy, who looks no more than eleven, joins them. He hugs all the girls in the group, who are twice the height of him, his ginger hair and freckles giving him the appearance of one of their younger brothers. But then one of them announces: 'You'd better sober up, Micko, or they won't let you in.'

One of the T-shirt-clad boys urinates against the newsagents' wall, while another young boy slowly grinds against his girlfriend as he leans her back against his chest, waiting for the nightclub to open. Yet another teen takes a long sip out of his can of Dutch Gold, oblivious to the bouncers on the door.

Later, across town, where a non-alcoholic disco is well under way, there is a controlled atmosphere as the gardai maintain a presence around the disco. Around 50 teenage boys squeeze their heads through the closed gates like caged animals in the zoo, desperately trying to get in to see the mini-skirted young girls who wait for them on the inside. The disco is full and the bouncers are no longer letting anyone else in. Demand for the event is so strong that tickets have actually been forged for it. One of the bouncers displays his find, they look so close to the

real thing that it's almost impossible to tell the difference.

It's a story that we have become accustomed to in the last few years: teenagers are hanging out in non-alcoholic discos but they're going into them inebriated. While we should never become immune to the sight of a drunken teenager, it's a sad fact that it simply isn't that shocking any more. We shrug our shoulders and say to each other that it wasn't like that in our day. However, when I was faced with the cold reality of what can happen, it's not so easy to adopt such a blasé attitude.

At 9pm, the time when most people are just setting out on their night out, the Junior Cert celebrations are already in full swing on another central street. I come across two young girls sitting on the steps near the bus station.

Originally I intended to ask them how they had done in their exams and how they were celebrating, but after the first few seconds it was clear that this didn't matter to either of them. One of them is sitting with her head lolling from side to side as her white Wonderbra pokes out of her top. Her skirt is hitched around her waist as she starts to cry.

Her friend, who is sober, is fighting back the tears as the second girl apologises. I had come across the two girls mid-debate over a ruined night, one too drunk to move, too drunk to think, too drunk to protect herself.

The drunk girl wants to stay around for another two hours. 'How long does it take to sober up?' she asks me pleadingly. She tells me that she had been drinking gin and vodka. Her friend adds that sometimes this had been with Coke, sometimes straight.

She hadn't been allowed into the nightclub because she was too drunk and her sober friend had drawn the short straw by staying with her.

A few hundred yards away, the rest of their friends are partying away in the basement of a hotel, oblivious as the two young girls sit on the steps.

The drunk girl had gone out to celebrate getting five As and four Bs in her Junior Cert. She was promised an iPod if she did well but now, coming home in this state she isn't sure if she's going to get it. This was the first time she had been drinking, she tells me.

As I try to persuade the girls to ring one of their mothers, a young man, a few years older, sits down on the step beside them. 'I have a boyfriend,' one of them immediately objects, but this man doesn't care. Seeing two young girls on the steps, one with her shoes thrown off, skirt hitched high and ladders in her tights, he sees an opportunity to pounce and he takes it. 'I'm not going anywhere,' he says, as he becomes increasingly aggressive. A group of his friends stroll by, but he remains, with no interest in what the rest of his friends are doing, just in trying to sidle up to the girls.

Then he offers the drunk girl some 'water' he was holding in a Volvic bottle. In her drunken state, she reaches out to take it until I intervene. Increasingly annoyed that his plans were being foiled, he stands up and delivers a barrage of abuse before eventually moving on. There is no one else on the streets, no one who could have helped them.

As soon as he leaves, the girl begins to vomit, the clear liquid pouring out of her lipstick-smudged mouth. Her mascara starts to run, leaving black tear marks on her face. 'I'm so sorry,' she repeats over and over to her friend. 'I'm sorry I ruined your night. Please don't ring my mum. Wait with me until twelve.'

Eventually, we ring her mother, who fortunately is just a ten-minute drive away. She pulls her car in across the road, marches over and hoists her daughter off the ground. Trying to stand up, she slips in her own vomit. 'That's it. You're not going out again until you're eighteen.'

The friend is left on her own, her friends don't have their phones, she tells me. I bring her down to the nightclub where her friends are, only to find the doors are shut. After I persuade one of the bouncers to let my 'little sister' in, she thankfully rejoins them.

Meanwhile, her friend is on the drive home with her mother, who barely even acknowledged my presence as a stranger, assisting her daughter. And the only apology she made was to the friend whose night was ruined. Perhaps she didn't realise that it could have been not just two little girls' nights, but their lives, that were ruined that night.

(Source: Sunday Independent, 18 September 2007)

1 What do you think of the teenagers' behaviour in this article?

2 Do you think it is unfair to stereotype teenagers in this way?

3 In what ways are the two girls putting their personal safety at risk?

4 Are there any dangers for teenage boys who drink heavily on a night out? What are they?

Class Discussion

Why do young people binge drink more than experienced drinkers?

 Useful Website

www.irishhealth.ie
www.mindbodyandsoul.gov.uk/alcohol
www.kidshealth.org
www.teens.drugabuse.gov

Module 10

Personal Safety

 Accidents at Home and at School

Accidents can and do happen, but most of them can be prevented. More accidents occur at home than anywhere else. There is no point in realising how accidents could have been prevented afterwards. To prevent accidents happening, possible risks and safety hazards must be identified and removed.

Class Discussion

Discuss some different accidents people in the class have had. How did they happen? Could they have been prevented?

 Useful Websites

www.lifebytes.gov.uk/safety
www.lifeguardsupport.co.uk
www.kidshealth.org/teen/safety
www.news.bbc.co.uk/cbbcnews
www.rsa.ie
www.watersafety.gov.kids

Group Work

List all the possible safety hazards in each room of the house. How can these hazards be removed or made safe?

Poster Task

Now that you have identified the safety hazards, design a safety in the home poster. The poster should contain all the precautions you can think of that will help prevent accidents.

 Fire Prevention

Fires in the home can be a major cause of death. Most house fires could be avoided and there is usually a simple method of prevention. It is hard to believe that something as simple as a phone charger, for example, could cause a fire.

Below is a list of some common causes of fires in the home. How could you ensure they are not a fire hazard? One has been done for you.

Cause of Fire	Prevention
Open fires	_Use a suitable fireguard_
Christmas lights left on	_____
Faulty sockets, wires and plugs	_____
Smouldering cigarettes	_____
Nightwear catching fire	_____
Lit candles	_____
Clothes near gas heaters	_____
Children using matches	_____
Unattended chip pan	_____
Chimney fire	_____
Phone chargers left plugged in	_____

 Fire Drill

Usually, when fire breaks out things can happen very quickly and panic can start; so it is important that your family has a rehearsed escape drill. It is important that a smoke alarm is fitted on each level of the house and this smoke alarm should be checked once a week.

Below is an example of an escape route. Draw a similar map of your own house and design the escape route.

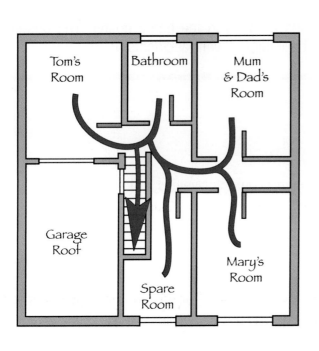
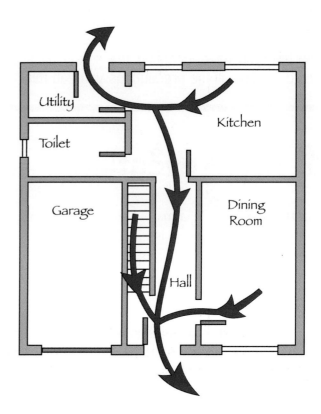

- **Ensure there are two escape routes.**
- **Practise the plan until perfected.**
- **Decide on a meeting point.**
- **Close all doors behind you as you leave.**
- **If you are caught in a smoke-filled room get down on your hands and knees.**
- **The stairs are your primary escape route – keep them clear.**
- **Never go back into the building.**
- **Call the fire brigade.**

(Source: National Safety Council)

Contacting the Emergency Services

- Dial 999 or 112.
- Tell the operator which service you require (fire, ambulance, gardai).
- Speak calmly and clearly.
- Give your address and phone number.
- Don't hang up until the operator tells you.

(Source: National Safety Council)

 # Water Safety

Every summer people set off to the beach or to rivers and lakes to cool off or to have fun. It is important to remember that every stretch of open water (beaches, ponds, rivers and lakes) has its own set of dangers. Before going swimming it's important to follow the water safety code:

1 spot the dangers

2 take advice

3 don't go it alone

4 learn how to help.

Spot the Dangers

Before going swimming you should spot any dangers and look out for any sources of information or help. For example, is there a lifeguard on duty, and if so, where is he/she? Are there any warning signs?

Write down other dangers you need to spot.

_____

_____

_____

_____

Take Advice

If the lifeguard is on duty ask him/her about possible dangers. Do not go swimming in a place you do not know. Look at the flags below: what do they mean?

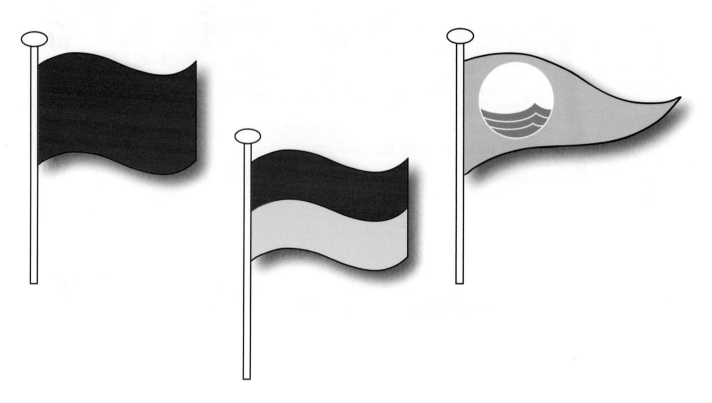

Don't go it Alone

Never swim on your own, and always tell someone where you are going.

Learn How to Help

- Call a lifeguard for help or get someone to dial 999.
- Throw a safety aid from the land to the person.
- If they are close reach out with a branch or an oar.
- Don't get in the water.

Below are fourteen steps to safe and enjoyable swimming that are issued by the Irish Water Safety Council. Match each picture with the relevant guideline.

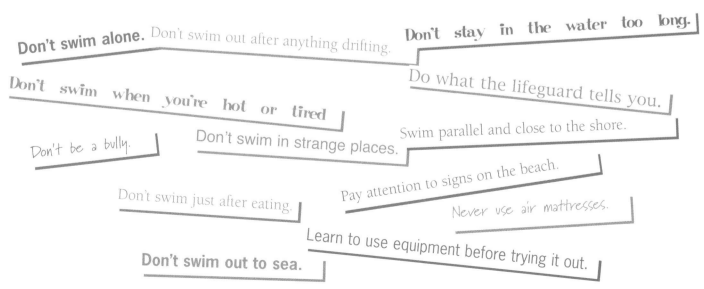

Don't swim alone. Don't swim out after anything drifting. **Don't stay in the water too long.**

Don't swim when you're hot or tired Do what the lifeguard tells you.

Don't be a bully. Don't swim in strange places. Swim parallel and close to the shore.

Don't swim just after eating. Pay attention to signs on the beach. Never use air mattresses.

Learn to use equipment before trying it out.

Don't swim out to sea.

First Aid

First aid is the first treatment given to a person who has been injured or taken ill. It is inevitable that accidents do happen; the important thing is to be prepared for when they do. A basic knowledge of first aid can be very helpful. There are many courses available throughout Ireland – why not find out about one in your area?

The aim of first aid is to:

- preserve life
- prevent the injury getting worse
- promote recovery.

The responsibilities of the first aider are:

- assess the situation, stay calm and act quickly
- make sure the area is safe for yourself and the casualty
- avoid moving the casualty unless the area they are in is unsafe
- do not place yourself in danger
- check for consciousness
- check for breathing
- check for pulse
- get help, phone for an ambulance or get someone else to (follow the steps for contacting the emergency services on p. 109).

Below are some examples of common injuries and their treatments. Practise each treatment in pairs.

 # Burns

There are three types of burn.

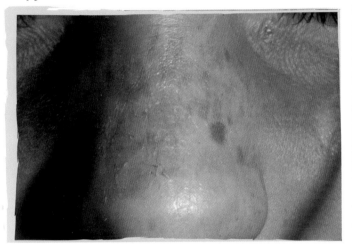
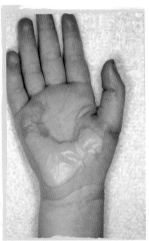
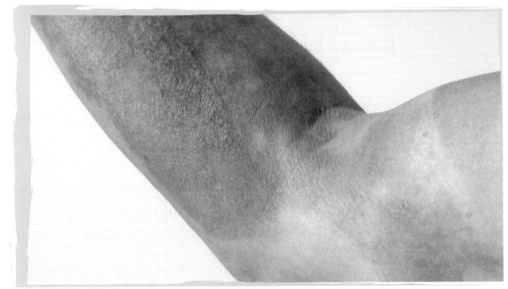

- First-degree burns – only the top layer of the skin is damaged. These burns are caused by brief contact with heat, which can cause redness and pain.
- Second-degree burns – the damage is deeper and usually causes blisters and redness.
- Third-degree burns – these are very deep burns. They may be painless initially and could need skin grafts.

Treatment

Anyone who suffers a second- or third-degree burn should go to hospital straight away.
If someone has a first- or second-degree burn and you cannot get them to hospital immediately:

- remove any clothing from around the area; but do not remove any clothing that is stuck to the skin
- run cool water over the burn for about ten minutes
- remove rings or watches, which may be difficult to remove if there is swelling in the area later
- apply a gauze bandage if it is a first-degree burn.

Do not:
- break blisters
- apply lotions, creams or ointments to large burned areas.

 # Treating Poisons

If you suspect someone has taken a poison and they are still conscious, you should:

- seek medical advice as soon as possible
- find out as much as possible about the poison they have taken
- bring a sample of the poison or the vomit to the hospital
- if the person has burns around the mouth and is *fully conscious*, give them a drink of milk.

Do not:
- make the casualty vomit.

Nosebleeds

Treatment:
- put on gloves
- lean the person's head forward
- pinch or get the person themselves to pinch the soft part of their nose
- apply pressure for about ten minutes
- advise the patient to breath through their mouth
- seek medical advice if bleeding occurs for longer than thirty minutes or if bleeding recurs.

Do not:
- tilt your head back
- blow your nose – and don't blow your nose for some hours.

Sprains and Strains

If you are unsure whether it is a sprain or a fracture you should treat it as a fracture.

Treatment for sprains and strains is RICE:

- *R – Rest* the injured muscle.
- *I – Ice.* Apply a cold compress for twenty minutes and keep reapplying; this helps to reduce swelling.
- *C – Compression.* Apply a firm bandage to reduce swelling.
- *E – Elevate.* Raise the injured area, to reduce blood flow.

→ Fainting

Fainting occurs when there is a lack of blood reaching the brain.

Treatment for someone who's feeling faint:

- Sit down and place the head between the knees.
- Loosen tight clothing.
- Advise the patient to take deep breaths.
- Allow patient to sit up slowly.
- Offer sips of water.
- Alternatively, get the person to lie down with their legs raised.

→ Cuts and Wounds

Most cuts can be easily treated at home but for deeper cuts and wounds which do not stop bleeding you should seek medical advice.

For minor cuts:

- Put on gloves.
- If the cut is dirty, clean it with a sterile wipe or run water over it.
- If there is a lot of bleeding, apply pressure to the wound until the bleeding stops.
- Raise the wounded area where necessary.
- Dress the affected area with a sterile pad and bandage.

Safety Quiz:

1 How often should you check the smoke alarm?

    a) Once a week

    b) Once a month

    c) Every six months

2 If a chip pan catches fire you should:

    a) Pour water over it

    b) Take it outside

    c) Place a fire blanket over it

3 A smoke alarm should be placed:

    a) In every room of the house

    b) In every level of the house

    c) In the hallway

4 A red flag on the beach means:

    a) It is safe to swim

    b) It is not safe to swim

    c) It is safe to surf

5 What should you do if you see someone in trouble on the beach?

    a) Dive in and rescue them

    b) Call for help then reach or throw something to them

    c) Run away to get someone.

6 If a person has a nose bleed you should:

    a) Get them to blow their nose

    b) Pinch their nose at the bridge and get them to tilt their nose forward

    c) Pinch the bridge and get them to tilt their head backwards

7 You should treat a first-degree burn by:

    a) Running it under cold water

    b) Placing cotton wool on the burn

    c) Put cream on it

Complete this module review in your copy after each module.

Module Review

Date:

In this module I learned about: _____

I enjoyed this module because: _____

I disliked this module because: _____

I would rate this module __ out of ten for relevance to my life. This module was relevant/not relevant to my life because:

_____

_____

_____

Crossword Solution

Crossword Solution

 Module 7: Sexual Reproduction Crossword

Across

8 Umbilical cord
9 Placenta
10 Crowning
11 Contractions
12 Fertilisation

Down

1 Unpasteurised
2 Folic acid
3 Fallopian tube
4 Amniotic
5 Nine
6 Carbon dioxide
7 Womb

Picture Credits